WITHDRAWN

W9-BYQ-287

CUTEST EVER BABY KNITS

3 1526 04139986 3

CUTEST EVER
BABY KNITS

VAL PIERCE

TRAFALGAR SQUARE
North Pomfret, Vermont

First published in the United States of America in 2011 by
Trafalgar Square Books
North Pomfret, VT 05053

Text copyright © 2011 Val Pierce
Copyright © 2011 New Holland Publishers (UK) Ltd

Val Pierce has asserted her moral right to be identified as the
author of this work.

All rights reserved. No part of this publication may be
reproduced, stored in a retrieval system, or transmitted in any
form or by any means, electronic, mechanical, photocopying,
recording or otherwise, without the prior written permission of
the publishers and copyright holders.

ISBN 978-1-57076-490-5
Library of Congress Control Number: 2011926121

Publisher: Clare Sayer
Senior editor: Marilyn Inglis
Photographer: Paul Bricknell
Additional technique photography: Mark Winwood
Designer: Isobel Gillan
Illustrator: Stephen Dew
Pattern checker: Tricia McKenzie
Production: Laurence Poos

10 9 8 7 6 5 4 3 2 1

Reproduction by Modern Age Repro House Ldt, Hong Kong

Printed and bound in Malaysia by Times Offset (M) Sdn Bhd

contents

introduction 6
with a little help... 8
let's get knitting 10

ballet-wrap cardigan 22
christening bib 27
nursery building blocks 30
bumble bee baby 33
doggie slippers 36
lemon sherbet sweater 39
flowers and squares blanket 44
sweet pea cardigan and hat 47
Edward Bear 52
berrylicious baby 56
baby blue booties 62
applique sleeping sack 65
shawl-collared jacket 71
strawberry shoes 76
teddy hoodie 79
nursery laundry bag 85
teddy bear hat 88
just rosy 92

suppliers 96

introduction

The art of knitting was once considered boring and old fashioned, but over the past few years this fascinating and relaxing hobby has seen a huge revival. Knitting clubs and groups have sprung up everywhere, and people from all walks of life have begun to learn or re-learn this wonderful craft. Enticed by the fabulous range of yarns and accompanying pattern books that are available these days, the would-be knitter has quite a dilemma when it comes to deciding what to make and which yarns to chose!

It is all too easy to go into a store and buy a ready-made garment but you will be missing out on the sheer pleasure of browsing the sumptuous yarns available, choosing just the right color and design for you or the person you are making it for. You will also miss out on the sheer satisfaction of spending some "me time" creating your own special work of art!

With this in mind I have designed a gorgeous range of baby knits to tempt even the novice knitter to create something wonderful for the special little one in your life. Designs range from traditional to contemporary and include sweet tops, cardigans and hats, to a rough-and-tumble Teddie hoodie, a warm shawl collar cardigan, doggy slippers and a cute bumble bee hat and mittens. There is also a snuggly blanket made in delicate spring shades, a useful toy or laundry bag, colorful play blocks and of course no nursery would be complete without an endearing teddy bear to cuddle.

All patterns are rated as to difficulty and there is something for most skill levels, from the beginner right through to the more experienced knitter who enjoys a challenge. The yarns used are all beautifully soft, practical and hand washable and are widely available throughout the UK, Europe and the US. There is a brief hints, tips and techniques section to get you started, which also includes useful conversion charts of needle sizes, yarn conversions and common knitting abbreviations.

Whatever your skill level and experience in knitting you are sure to find some project within that will inspire you to get busy with your needles.

Happy knitting!

with a little help...

Hints, tips and techniques to get you started – including a quick run-down of basic stitches, working with color and charts, and completing your project.

MATERIALS AND ACCESSORIES

Yarns

It can be quite intimidating for a new knitter to decide which yarns to use for a project. The choice available these days is quite stunning and ranges from naturals to synthetics, alpaca, metallic, cashmere, silk, blends of wool and acrylic, to name but a few. They come in different thicknesses or weight: fine yarns such as 2- and 3-ply, for instance, are normally used for baby garments and shawls. Probably the most widely used yarns are 4-ply and double knitting weight, then we come to Aran and chunky weight yarns that knit up quickly and produce heavyweight garments. All the projects in the book have specified yarns but you can substitute these for different yarns as long as you check your gauge before beginning the work and you keep to the same ply or weight recommended in the pattern. If you do decide to change yarns then it is possible that you will achieve a different look to your finished garment than that of the design.

Accessories

Before embarking on your first garment you need to acquire a few basic tools. There are many brands of knitting needles available these days, and the price range is varied. It is wise to invest in some good-quality needles since these will give you many years of service. A tape measure, stitch holders, row markers, cable needle, a good sharp pair of needlework scissors and a range of sewing up needles are recommended too. A knitting bag is also a very handy thing in which to store your work in progress; not only does it keep your work clean while you are knitting, you can store the patterns and yarns you are using all in one place ready to begin work.

let's get knitting

The next pages outline the basic methods of casting on and binding off, knit and purl stitches, increasing and decreasing, as well as working in color and from charts.

CASTING ON AND BINDING OFF

There are several methods for casting on and binding off. Some knitting patterns will stipulate a particular method, depending on the effect required within the pattern – it is common to bind off in pattern, for instance. Make sure your cast on and bind off stitches remain elastic by either working them loosely or using a larger size needle than stated if you think you work very tightly. Most patterns will tell you which side of the knitting to finish your work on but as a general rule most binding off is done with the right side of the work facing.

Casting on – two-needle method

This method involves creating a row of loops cast on to a needle. The second needle is used to build a series of interjoining loops in a row. Hold the needle with the stitches in your left hand and the needle to make the stitches in your right hand. (If you are left-handed, do the reverse) To start, make a slip knot about 4 in (10 cm) from the end of your yarn, slip it over the needle in your left hand. Then insert the right-hand needle through the front loop as if you were making a knit stitch (now follow steps 1–4).

1 Pass the yarn under and over the point of the right-hand needle (again as if you were making a knit stitch).

2 Using the right-hand needle, draw the yarn through the slip knot to form a new stitch.

3 Transfer new stitch to left-hand needle, insert right-hand needle through front of new stitch and repeat 1.

4 Continue in this way until you have cast on the required number of stitches specified in your pattern.

Casting on – one-needle or thumb method

1 Making sure that you have unwound sufficient yarn from the main ball to allow you to cast on the stated number of stitches, make a slip knot and place it on the needle.

2 Wind the yarn clockwise around your thumb and hold firmly. Insert the point of the needle through the loop on your thumb.

3 Wind the yarn in your left hand around the back of the point of the needle and in between the needle and your thumb. Pull the point of the needle under the yarn to form a stitch.

4 Slip the stitch on to the needle close to the slip knot. Continue in this way until you have the required number of stitches specified in your pattern.

Binding off

The technique of binding off is used to provide the finished edge to the end of your work. It is also used when you shape pieces or make buttonholes. It is normal to bind off on the right side of your work; however, follow the instructions since you may have to bind off in pattern. Don't pull stitches too tightly when binding off, since this may result in a puckered edge, or make it difficult when sewing up the seams of the garment.

1 Work the first two stitches in pattern. With the yarn at the back of the work, insert the point of the needle through the first stitch.

2 Using the left-hand needle, lift the first stitch over the second stitch and then off the needle.

3 Work the next stitch in pattern. Once again using the left-hand needle, lift the first stitch over the second stitch and off the needle.

4 Continue to do this all the way along the row until left with a single stitch. Slip this off the needle and pull the end of the yarn through it firmly to secure it.

KNIT AND PURL STITCHES

To create any fabric when beginning to knit there are two fundamental stitches that need to be learned and mastered. The knit stitch is the first stitch normally learned when beginning to knit; this forms a ridged fabric known as garter stitch and can be widely used for many projects. The second stitch needed is a purl stitch, which when teamed with the knit stitch creates what we call stockinette stitch; this results in a fabric that is smooth on the right side and ridged on the wrong side. Once you have mastered these two stitches, the sky is the limit. They can be used to work many beautiful patterns and decorative stitches and are the basis for all knitting. But just to make things more interesting, there are several different methods of achieving these basic stitches.

Knit stitch – English/American method

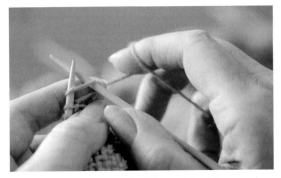

1 Hold the needle with cast-on stitches in your left hand, wind the yarn around the little finger of your right hand, then under the two middle fingers and over the top of your forefinger.

2 Keeping the yarn at the back of the work, hold the second needle in your right hand and insert it into the front of the first stitch.

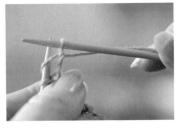

3 With your right forefinger, bring the yarn forward, under and over the point of the right-hand needle.

4 Pull the yarn through the loop and push the resulting stitch towards the point of the left-hand needle.

5 Slip it on to the right-hand needle.

Knit stitch – Continental method

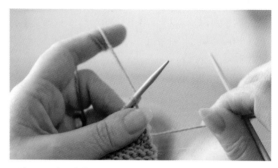

1 Hold needle with cast-on stitches in your right hand, wind the yarn over your left forefinger and lay it across the palm of your hand, then take up slack between your two last fingers.

2 Place work in left hand, extend left forefinger, pulling yarn behind the needle. Use left thumb and middle finger to push first stitch towards point and insert right-hand needle.

3 Twist right needle and place point under the working yarn to pull the loop onto the right-hand needle.

4 It may help to hold loop with right forefinger while you pull it down through the stitch. Pull new stitch on right-hand needle.

Purl stitch – English/American method

1 Holding needle with cast-on stitches in your left hand, wind yarn around your little finger, under your middle fingers and over the forefinger of right hand.

2 With yarn in the front of the work, pick up the needle in your right hand and insert the point into the front of the first stitch on left-hand needle.

3 With your right forefinger, wind yarn around the point of the right-hand needle and then under it.

4 Pull loop on right needle through stitch and push new stitch towards point of left needle; slip stitch to right needle.

Purl stitch – Continental method

1 Take the yarn over your left forefinger, lay it across your palm and take up the slack between your last two fingers. Then hold the work in your left hand.

2 Push out left forefinger slightly, pulling working yarn in front of needle. Using your left thumb and forefinger, push the first stitch towards the point of left-hand needle.

3 Insert right needle into front of stitch. Use left forefinger to wind yarn around right-hand needle.

4 Push down and back with right needle to pull loop through stitch and slip on to right-hand needle.

INCREASING AND DECREASING

When working on some projects it is necessary to shape the pieces as you work. In order to do this you will need to lose or gain stitches on the rows as you knit. This is done by either increasing the number of stitches (done by knitting twice into the same stitch), or decreasing (achieved by knitting two stitches together). There are quite a few ways of doing this but most patterns will state clearly which method is recommended.

Increasing – bar method

1 Knit a stitch in the usual way but do not take it off the left-hand needle.

2 Insert the point of the right-hand needle into the back of the same stitch (part of which remains on the left-hand needle)...

3 and knit again. Take the stitch from the left needle to the right in the usual way.

4 The extra stitch formed by this method produces a small bump on the right side of the work and is not too noticeable when worked on the edge of a garment.

Decreasing – right slant (k2tog)

1 Insert the needle in the next two stitches, through the front of both loops. Wind the yard around the needle in the usual way and pull it through.

2 Transfer the new stitch on to the right-hand needle, again in the usual way.

Decreasing – left slant (k2tog tbl)

1 Insert the needle in the next two stitches through the back of both loops. Wind the yarn around the needle.

2 Pull the yarn through and transfer the new stitch on to the right-hand needle.

Decreasing – slip stitch decrease

1 Slip one stitch knitwise from the left-hand needle on to the right-hand needle, then knit the next stitch.

2 Insert the left-hand needle into the front of the slipped stitch and pull it over the knitted one.

3 The right-to-left slant made by this decrease in a knit row is used on the right side of the center of the work.

PICKING UP STITCHES

Some of the designs in the book have neckbands and front bands knitted on to them, which entails picking up stitches along an already knitted edge. Use a smaller size needle than the one you are going to continue with, since this makes the process easier. Do not pick up stitches at the very edge of the knitting; picking up the stitches that lie one stitch in from the edge will result in a much neater finish. Always try to ensure that stitches are picked up evenly along the edge or neckband when working.

Joining new yarns

Never join new yarn in the middle of a row – it makes for an uneven bump in the fabric and can result in a hole if the ends work loose.

1 Hold the working yarn behind the completed piece, and insert the needle through it, between the rows and between the last two stitches of each row, from front to back.

2 Wind yarn over the needle as if you were going to knit a stitch then pull a loop of yarn through to form a stitch. Continue until the required number of stitches is formed.

WORKING WITH TWO OR MORE COLORS

A couple of the designs in the book use more than one color in a row. When working these it is advisable to use the stranding method whereby you carry the yarn not in use fairly loosely across the back of the work as you knit. The yarn can be tied into the work on every third of fourth stitch to keep the work neat and elastic. Care must be taken not to pull yarn too tightly when doing this otherwise it will result in puckering of the fabric.

Working from a chart

Color patterns are often charted on graph paper. Each square represents a stitch and each horizontal line of squares is a row of stitches. Some charts are colored in while others are simply black and white and have a key at the side with different symbols depicting different shades. Charts are read from bottom to top and usually from right to left. They are normally in stockinette stitch and odd numbered rows will be knit and even numbered rows will be purl.

Adding new yarn at the beginning of a row

1 Insert the right-hand needle into the first stitch on the left-hand need and wind both old and new yarns over it. Knit the stitch with both yarns.

2 Drop the old yarn and pick up the new, then knit the next two stitches with the short end and the working yarn.

3 Drop the short end of the new yarn and continue knitting in pattern.

4 On subsequent row, purl the three double stitches in the normal way.

Adding new yarn within a row

1 With old yarn at the back of the work, insert the point of right needle into the stitch. Wind new yarn over needle and use it as your new stitch.

2 Knit the next two stitches with both the new and old colors.

3 Drop short end and continue knitting with new yarn while carrying old yarn across the back. On subsequent rows purl the double stitches normally.

Therefore the first stitch of a chart is the bottom one on the right. Placing a straight edge of some kind under each row will help you keep your place in the chart when working the design.

Intarsia

This is another method of adding color to your work, and is for the more experienced knitter. The motif or patterning is normally written onto a chart for you follow row by row and the yarns used are not taken across the back of the work as in stranding, but each individual area of color is knitted using a separate piece of yarn. Winding small lengths of color onto bobbins or small pieces of card helps to eliminate tangling when using different colors in the same row.

Making bobbles

When making a bobble in the pattern you will need to knit into the front and back of the stated stitch the required number of times. You will then work back and forth on these stitches as stated; the final row decreases the added stitches and results in a bobble in your work. When you purl the next row, work firmly, thus pushing the bobble to the front of

work and closing up any gaps that have been made.

Gauge

It is very important to check your gauge before you start any project as it will have an effect on your finished garment. Remember, if you get fewer stitches to the inch (centimeter) than stated, your gauge is too loose and a smaller needle is required. If you get

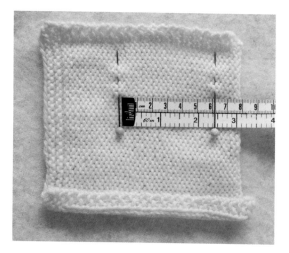

more stitches to the inch (centimeter) than stated your gauge is too tight and a larger needle will be required. When measuring your gauge don't stretch the work out to make it fit or vice versa; knit up one or two samples until you get it just right.

Measurements and measuring

Most of the garments within this book are designed so there will be an allowance for a comfortable fit. When measuring pieces of knitting while working on your project it is much easier and more reliable to count the number of rows you have knitted. Sleeves and side seams will all line up and fit much better if the rows are the same. Sewing in sleeves sometimes causes problems, but if you pin and ease the sleeve in place before stitching you should get a good result. Raglan sleeves are easier to stitch in since they lay flat when sewing.

COMPLETING YOUR PROJECT

Correcting mistakes

It is inevitable that you will make the occasional mistake in your work. Checking back at regular intervals is always a good idea, and should the need arise to correct errors, there will not be too many rows to unpick or unravel. A dropped stitch can often be picked up with the aid of a crochet hook and worked back up the piece of knitting a row at a time. If you need to unravel work then do it slowly and carefully, using a smaller size needle to pick up the stitches from the unravelled row, and change back to the correct size needle to begin working again. It is very difficult to pick up dropped stitches in lacy work so take extra care when working these type of designs.

Making a twisted cord

Take two lengths of yarn and fold into a double strand. To measure the amount you need, keep in mind that when folded and twisted your original length will end up a quarter of its length. Tie a knot in each end of yarn, insert a pencil in one end and secure the other to a doorknob. Twist the pencil until yarn is tightly twisted, keeping it tight at all times. Fold yarn in half and let it twist on itself, then even it out and tie the other end firmly to stop it untwisting.

Finishing

After completing your work of art you will need to finish it. Always read the ball band of the yarn you have used, since this will give you details about pressing and washing your garment.

Sewing the pieces together sometimes seems difficult for novice knitters but if you work methodically and carefully you will find it is quite simple. There are many seams to chose from depending on the type of yarn used and the garment you have made. Back stitch gives a neat little ridge on the inside of the work. You can also work from the front of the knitting, laying the pieces to be sewn up on a flat surface so that you can catch adjacent stitches together, one from each piece as you sew. This is tricky to begin with but once the technique is mastered it gives an almost invisible seam, and makes matching patterns and stripes a lot easier. Take care to stretch front bands slightly when sewing them on as this gives a firmer and more professional finish to cardigans. Most patterns will give instructions on finishing a particular garment for you to follow.

THE LANGUAGE OF KNITTING

Listed below are some common knitting terms and meanings. Some patterns contain abbreviations specific to that pattern and are listed on the page.

k knit
p purl
k2tog knit 2 stitches together, decreasing a stitch
p2tog purl 2 stitches together, decreasing a stitch
st(s) stitch(es)
tog together
tbl through back of loop(s)
inc increase by working into front and back of stitch
dec decrease by working 2 stitches together
beg beginning
alt alternate
rep repeat
foll following
rem remain(ing)
RS right side
WS wrong side
sl1 k or p slip 1 knitways or purlwise
yf yarn forward
yfrn yarn in front and round needle
yrn yarn round needle
yo yarn over needle
psso pass slipped stitch over
patt pattern
M1 make a stitch by picking up horizontal loop lying before next stitch and working into back of it
yb yarn to back of work
st st stockinette stitch

Crochet terms
sl st slip stitch
ch chain
dc US single crochet/double crochet
tr US double crochet/treble crochet

NEEDLES SIZE CONVERSIONS

Metric (mm)	US	UK
2 mm	0	14
2¼ mm	1	13
2¾ mm	2	12
3 mm	2/3	11
3¼ mm	3	10
3¾ mm	5	9
4 mm	6	8
4½ mm	7	7
5 mm	8	6
5½ mm	9	5
6 mm	10	4
6½ mm	10½	3
7 mm	10½	2
7½ mm	11	1
8 mm	11	0
9 mm	13	00
10 mm	15	000

YARN CONVERSIONS

US	UK/AUSTRALIA
lace weight	1 ply
baby	2 ply
fingering	3 ply
sport weight	4 ply
worsted weight	8 ply, double knit, dk
fisherman or medium	10 ply, Aran
bulky	12 ply, chunky

ballet-wrap cardigan

Cream and pale lilac are a lovely combination for a sweet little ballet-wrap cardigan. The sleeves are plain while the back and front are worked in an eyelet and bobble pattern. The front bands are worked as an integral part of each front.

♥♥ Intermediate

∙∙

MEASUREMENTS
To fit newborn–3 month old baby
Chest 18 in (46 cm); length 7½ in (19 cm);
sleeve length 6 in (15 cm)

MATERIALS
- Sirdar Snuggly DK 45% acrylic/55% nylon (50 g balls; 191 yd/175 m): 1 x 50 g ball shade 219 Lilac; 2 x 50 g balls shade 303 Cream
- Knitting needles size US 5 (UK 9/3¾ mm)
- 2 x lilac buttons
- ½ yard (½ m) lilac baby ribbon

GAUGE
22 sts x 30 rows measures 4 in (10 cm) square over st st

SPECIAL ABBREVIATIONS
MB = Make bobble. K1, p1, k1, p1, k1 all into next st to make 5 sts, turn and purl 5, turn, pass 2nd, 3rd, 4th and 5th sts one at a time over first st, then knit into the back of this st.

∙∙

SLEEVES
Make two alike.
Using US 5 (UK 9/3¾ mm) needles and lilac yarn cast on 32 sts. Change to cream yarn and work in k1 p1 rib for 10 rows.
Change to st st and inc 1 st at each end of 5th and every following 6th row until there are 42 sts on needle. Continue in st st without shaping until work measures 6 in (15 cm) ending on a purl row.
Shape top
Bind off 3 sts at beg of next 2 rows (36 sts).
Next row: K1, sl1, k1, psso, knit to last 3 sts, k2tog, k1.
Next row: K1, purl to last st, k1.
Repeat last 2 rows until 6 sts remain. Bind off.

BACK
Using US 5 (UK 9/3¾ mm) needles and lilac yarn cast on 57 sts. Change to cream yarn and work in k1 p1 rib for 10 rows.
Change to st st and work pattern as follows:
Rows 1–4: Work in st st.
Row 5: K3, *yf, sl1, k1, psso, k8*, repeat from * to * to last 5 sts, yf, sl1, k1, psso, k2.
Row 6: Purl.
Row 7: K1, *k2tog, yf, k1, yf, sl1, k1, psso, k5*, repeat from * to * to last 6 sts, k2tog, yf, k1, yf, sl1, k1, psso, k1.

Row 8: Purl.

Row 9: K3, MB, *k9, MB*, repeat from * to * to last 3 sts, k3.

Row 10: Purl.

Rows 11–14: Work in st st.

Row 15: K8. *yf, sl1, k1, psso, k8*, repeat from * to * to last 9 sts, yf, sl1, k1, psso, k7 .

Row 16: Purl.

Row 17: K6, *k2tog, yf, k1, yf, sl1, k1, psso, k5*, repeat from * to * to last st, k1.

Row 18: Purl.

Row 19: K8, MB, *k9, MB*, repeat from * to * to last 8 sts, k8.

Row 20: Purl.

Note: The last 20 rows set the pattern repeat.

Shape armholes

Keeping pattern correct, bind off 3 sts at beg of next 2 rows (51 sts).

Next row: K1, sl1, k1, psso, pattern to last 3 sts, k2tog, k1.

Next row: K1, purl to last st, k1.

Repeat last 2 rows until 29 sts remain.

Next row: K1, sl1, k1, psso, pattern to last 3 sts, k2tog, k1.

Next row: K1, p2tog, pattern to last 3 sts, p2tog tbl, k1.

Repeat last 2 rows until 13 sts remain. Bind off.

RIGHT FRONT

Using US 5 (UK 9/3¾ mm) needles and lilac yarn cast on 38 sts. Change to cream yarn and proceed:

Row 1: K5 (p1, k1) to last st, p1.

Row 2: (K1, p1) to last 4 sts, k4.

Repeat last 2 rows once more.

Row 5: K5, (p1, k1) 5 times, p1, yrn, p2tog, k1, (p1, k1) 9 times, p1.

Repeat row 2 once and then rows 1 and 2 twice more.

Now work pattern and shape front as follows:

Row 1: Knit.

Row 2: Purl to last 4 sts, k4.

Row 3: K4, sl1, k1 psso, knit to end (37 sts).

Row 4: Purl to last 4 sts, k4.

Row 5: K13, (yf, sl1, k1, psso, k8) twice, yf, sl1, k1, psso, k2.

Row 6: Purl to last 4 sts, k4.

Row 7: K4, sl1, k1, psso, (k5, k2tog, yf, k1, yf, sl1, k1, psso) 3 times, k1 (36 sts).

Row 8: Purl to last 4 sts, k4.

Row 9: K12, MB, (k9, MB) twice, k3.

Row 10: Purl to last 4 sts, k4.

Row 11: K4, sl1, k1, psso, knit to end (35 sts).

Row 12: Purl to last 4 sts, k4.

Row 13: Knit.

Row 14: Purl to last 4 sts, k4.

Row 15: K4, sl1, k1, psso, K10, yf, sl1, k1, psso, k8, yf, sl1, k1, psso, k7 (34 st).

Row 16: Purl to last 4 sts, k4

Row 17: K13, (k2tog, yf, k1, yf, sl1, k1, psso, k5) twice, k1.

Row 18: Purl to last 4 sts, k4.

Row 19: K4, sl1, k1, psso, (k9, MB) twice, k8 (33 sts).

Row 20: Purl to last 4 st, k4.

Note: The last 20 rows set the pattern repeat.

Shape armholes

Next row: Knit.

Next row: Bind off 3 sts, purl to end (30 sts).

Next row: K4, sl1, k1, psso, pattern to last 3 sts, k2tog, k1.

Next row: K1, purl to last 4 sts, k4.

Keeping pattern correct, decreasing at armhole on alt rows and front inside edge on every 4th row as before, work until 25 sts remain, ending on a WS row.

Next row: K2, yf, k2tog, pattern to last 3 sts, k2 tog, k1.
Next row: K1, purl to last 4 sts, k4.
Continue decreasing at armhole and front inside edge as before until 13 sts remain, ending on a WS row.
Next row: K10, k2tog, k1.
Next row: K1, p2tog, purl to last 4 sts, k4.
Next row: K4, sl1, k1, psso, k2, k2tog, k1.
Next row: K1, p2tog, p2, k4.
Next row: K5, k2tog, k1.
Next row: K1, p2tog, k4.
Next row: K4, k2tog.
Next row: K2tog, k3 (4 sts).
Work 16 rows in garter stitch on these 4 sts. Bind off.

LEFT FRONT

Using US 5 (UK 9/3¾ mm) needles and lilac yarn cast on 38 sts. Change to cream yarn and proceed:
Row 1: (P1, k1) to last 4 sts, k4.
Row 2: K4, (p1, k1) to end.
Repeat last 2 rows 4 times more. Now work pattern and shape front slope as follows:
Row 1: Knit.
Row 2: K4, purl to end.
Row 3: Knit to last 6 sts, k2tog, k4 (37 sts).
Row 4: K4, purl to end.
Row 5: K3, (yf, sl1, k1, psso, k8) 3 times, k4.
Row 6: K4, purl to end.
Row 7: K1, (k2tog, yf, k1, yf, sl1, k1, psso, k5) 3 times, k2tog, k4 (36 sts).
Row 8: K4 purl to end.
Row 9: K3, (MB, k9) twice, MB, k12.
Row 10: K4, purl to end.
Row 11: Knit to last 6 sts, k2tog, k4 (35 sts).
Row 12: K4, purl to end.
Row 13: Knit.

Row 14: K4, purl to end.
Row 15: (K8, yf, sl1, k1, psso) twice, k9, k2tog, k4 (34 sts).
Row 16: K4, purl to end.
Row 17: K6, (k2tog, yf, k1, yf, sl1, k1, psso, k5) twice, k8.
Row 18: K4, purl to end.
Row 19: K8, (MB, k9) twice, k2tog, k4 (33 sts).
Row 20: K4, purl to end.
Note The last 20 rows set the pattern repeat.

Shape armhole
Next row: Bind off 3 sts, pattern to end (30 sts).
Next row: K4, purl to last st, k1.
Next row: K1, sl1, k1, psso, patt to last 6 sts, k2tog, k4.
Next row: K4, purl to last st, k1.
Keeping pattern correct, decreasing at armhole on alt rows and front inside edge on every 4th row as before, work until 13 sts remain, ending on a WS row.
Next row: K1, sl1, k1, psso, k10.
Next row: K4, p5, p2tog tbl, k1.
Next row: K1, sl1, k1, psso, k2, k2tog, k4.
Next row: K4, p2, p2tog tbl, k1.
Next row: K1, sl1, k1, psso, k5.
Next row: K4, p2tog tbl, k1.
Next row: Sl1, k1, psso, k4.
Next row: K3, k2tog, tbl (4 st).
Work 16 rows in garter stitch on these 4 sts. Bind off.

TO FINISH

Work in ends on all pieces. Join raglan seams neatly. Join front bands and stitch to remaining neck edge. Join side and sleeve seams. Attach ribbons and buttons to correspond with button holes.

christening bib

White cotton-mix yarn is used to make this gorgeous baby bib ideal for special occasions. A pretty stitch pattern and ribbon motif add delicate charm to the finished project. I've used white but you can choose your own favorites.

♥ Beginner

MEASUREMENTS
To fit newborn–3 month old baby

MATERIALS
- Sirdar Calico DK 60% cotton/40% acrylic (50 g balls; 172 yd/158 m): 1 x 50 g ball shade Cotton White 723
- Ribbon rose motif
- Knitting needles size US 6 (UK 8/4 mm)
- Stitch markers

GAUGE
22 sts x 28 rows measures 4 in (10 cm) square over st st

SPECIAL ABBREVIATIONS
SS = seed stitch (UK moss stitch). Created by alternately working 1 knit stitch and 1 purl stitch on every row. The purl stitch is worked over the knit stitch on the subsequent row.

BIB
Using US 6 (UK 8/4 mm) needles, cast on 44 sts.
Work 4 rows in SS (seed stitch) as follows:
Row 1: *K1, p1*, repeat from * to * to end.
Row 2: *P1, k1*, repeat from * to * to end.
Repeat rows 1 and 2 once more.
Keeping 3 sts either end in SS, work diamond pattern as follows:
Note: Use a marker either side of the 3 edge stitches.
Row 1 (RS): SS 3, p4, *k1, p8*, rep from * to * to last 8 sts, k1, p4, SS 3.
Row 2: SS 3, k3, *p3, k6*, rep from * to * to last 9 sts, p3, k3, SS 3.
Row 3: SS 3, p2, *k5, p4*, rep from * to * to last 10 sts, k5, p2, SS 3.
Row 4: SS 3, k1, *p7, k2*, rep from * to * to last 11 sts, p7, k1, SS 3.
Row 5: SS 3, knit to last 3 sts, SS 3.
Row 6: As row 4.
Row 7: As row 3.
Row 8: As row 2.
Repeat these 8 rows once more.
Now work across all sts in SS as before for 4 rows.
Next row: SS 3, knit to last 3 sts, SS 3.
Next row: SS 3, purl to last 3 sts, SS 3.
Continue as set on the last 2 rows for a further 20 rows.
Now work across all stitchs in SS as before for 4 rows.

Shape top and ties

Next row: SS 13 sts, bind off 16 sts, SS to end.

Keeping SS pattern correct, work on first set of 13 sts as follows:

Next row: Dec 1 st at each end of row.

Next row: Dec 1 st at beg of row, work to end.

Next 2 rows: Dec 1 st at each end of row.

Next row: Dec 1 st at beg of row, work to end (5 sts).

Continue on these 5 sts for a further 6 in (15 cm). Bind off.

With wrong side facing, return to remaining 13 sts, rejoin yarn and complete second side and tie to match other side, reversing shapings.

TO FINISH

Work in ends neatly. Fold each tie in half lengthwise and stitch together for 4¾ in (12 cm). Attach ribbon motif very securely to front of bib.

nursery building blocks

Bright colors and smiley faces make these soft building blocks ideal for your baby. Little fingers can hold, explore and learn to build. Using small amounts of yarn from your stash, you can knit a block in just a few hours.

♥ Beginner

MEASUREMENTS
4 in (10 cm) cubes

MATERIALS
- Patons Fairytale Color 4 Me DK 100% wool (50 g balls; 198 yd/90 m) in the following shades:
  1 x 50 g ball 4957 Aqua; 1 x 50 g ball 4953 Pink;
  1 x 50 g ball 4952 Green; 1 x 50 g ball 4960 Yellow;
  1 x 50 g ball 4967 Red; 1 x 50 g ball 4955 Blue;
  1 x 50 g ball 4951 Orange; small amount of black yarn for embroidery
- Knitting needles size US 5 (UK 9/3¾ mm)
- Knitting needles size US 3 (UK 10/3¼ mm)
- Fiberfill stuffing or foam blocks 4 in (10 cm) square

GAUGE
22 sts and 30 rows measures 4 in (10 cm) square over st st.
Gauge is not critical if you accept a slight variation in size of the finished project. You will need 6 squares to make 1 building block.

SPECIAL ABBREVIATIONS
SS = seed stitch (UK moss stitch). See page 27 for description of this stitch.

BLOCKS

Using the color of your choice and US 5 (UK 9/3¾ mm) needles cast on 25 sts. Work 4 rows (SS) seed stitch as follows:

Row 1: K1, *p1, k1*, rep from * to * to end.
Row 2: K1, *p1, k1*, rep from * to * to end.
Repeat these 2 rows once more.
Keeping 4 sts either end in SS, work patt as follows:
Row 1: SS 4, knit 17, SS 4.
Row 2: SS 4, purl 17, SS 4.
Repeat these 2 rows 11 times more.
Now work across all sts in SS as before for 4 rows.
Bind off in pattern. This completes one side of the block. You need to make a further 5 pieces in different shades to complete your block.

SMILEY FACES
Using US 3 (UK 10/3¼ mm) needles and color of your choice cast on 55 sts.
Knit 1 row.
Now work pattern as follows:
Row 1: K4, sl1, k2tog, psso, *k8, sl1, k2tog, psso*, repeat from * to * to last 4 sts, k4.
Row 2: K3, sl1, k2tog, psso, *k6, sl1, k2tog, psso*, repeat from * to * to last 3 sts, k3.

Row 3: K2, sl1, k2tog, psso, *k4, sl1, K2tog, psso*, repeat from * to * to last 2 sts, k2.

Row 4: K1, sl1, k2tog, psso, *k2, sl1, k2tog, psso*, repeat from * to * to last st, k1.

Row 5: *Sl1, k2tog, psso*, repeat from * to * to end (5 sts).

Break yarn and run through remaining sts, draw up tight and secure, stitch side seam of face.

With black yarn stitch a smiley face, using the photograph as a guide.

TO FINISH

With right sides of squares facing, lay two pieces side by side, stitch together on the right sides of work, matching rows as you do. Take a blunt-ended needle and sew through the tiny "bumps" of the garter stitch on adjacent rows. Pull together quite firmly and the seam will be almost invisible.

Join the rest of the squares to form a cube shape. Before closing the final seam, either stuff or insert a ready-cut foam block. Sew smiley faces to one or two sides of the block.

bumble bee baby

Get busy with your needles and make this really cute hat and cozy mittens for your little one. The yarn is soft merino wool in vibrant shades of black and yellow. If you don't like the strong colors, choose different shades.

♥♥ Intermediate

MEASUREMENTS
To fit 3–6 month old baby

MATERIALS
- Rico Essentials Merino Wool 100% pure machine washable (50 g balls; 130 yd/120 m) in the following shades: 1 x 50 g ball shade 90 Black; 2 x 50 g balls shade 66 Sun Yellow
- Small oddment of cream DK yarn for wings
- Knitting needles size US 5 (UK 9/3¾ mm)
- Double-pointed knitting needles size US 5 (UK 9/3¾ mm)

GAUGE
22 sts x 28 rows measures 4 in (10 cm) square over st st

SPECIAL ABBREVIATION
M1 = Make a stitch by picking up the strand of yarn between stitches and knitting into the back of it.

HAT

Using US 5 (UK 9/3¾ mm) needles and black yarn cast on 84 sts.

Work 6 rows in garter stitch.

Now work pattern as follows:

Join in yellow and proceed in st st stripes of 6 rows yellow/2 rows black until you have worked 26 rows in total, thus ending on a purl row.

Note: After finishing the fourth yellow stripe, continue in black only to complete the hat.

Now proceed to shape the top as follows:

Row 1: K3, (k2tog, k4) 13 times, k2tog, k1.

Row 2: Purl.

Row 3: K2, (k2tog, k3) 13 times, k2tog, k1.

Row 4: Purl.

Row 5: K1, (k2tog, k2) 13 times, k2tog, k1.

Row 6: Purl.

Row 7: (K2tog, k1) 14 times.

Row 8: Purl.

Row 9: (K2tog) 14 times (7 sts).

Break yarn, run through remaining sts, draw up tight and secure.

To make antenna

Using two double-pointed needles and black yarn cast on 7 sts and work an I-cord for approximately 6½ in (16 cm). See instructions opposite. Bind off.

MITTS

Make two alike.

Using US 5 (UK 9/3¾ mm) needles and black yarn cast on 33 sts. Work 4 rows in garter stitch.

Now work pattern as follows:

Join in yellow and proceed in st st stripes of 6 rows yellow/2 rows black until you have completed the third black stripe, thus ending on a purl row.

To make an I-cord

An I-cord is a narrow piece of knitting made on double-pointed needles. Although the method sounds a bit complicated, you will find it is very simple and quick to do. Using double-pointed needles and stated yarn cast on required number of stitches (see antenna pattern opposite). Knit the first row. Slide the stitches to the opposite end of the needle. The working yarn is at the bottom of the row. Knit again, pulling the working yarn up the back of the piece so you can knit with it. Again slide the stitches to the opposite end of the needle. Repeat in this manner. As you pull the yarn the back will close up on itself, like magic. Continue until the piece measures the required length.

Now start shaping top as follows:

Row 1: K1, (sl1, k1, psso, k11, k2tog, k1) twice (29 sts).

Row 2 (and following wrong side rows): Purl.

Row 3: K1, (sl1, k1, psso, k9, k2tog, k1) twice (25 sts).

Row 5: K1, (sl1, k1, psso, k7, k2tog, k1) twice (21 sts).

Break yellow yarn and continue in black yarn only.

Row 7: K1, (sl1, k1, psso, k5, k2tog, k1) twice 17 sts).

Row 8: Purl.

Bind off.

Wings

Make four alike.

Using US 5 (UK 9/3¾ mm) needles and cream yarn cast on 5 sts.

Row 1: Knit.

Row 2: K2, M1 (by picking up the strand of yarn between the stitches and knitting into the back of it), k1, M1, k2 (7 sts).

Row 3 (and following alternate rows): Knit.

Row 4: K3, M1, k1, M1, k3 (9 sts).

Row 6: K4, M1, k1, M1, k4 (11 sts).

Rows 8 and 10: Knit

Row 12: K2tog, knit to last 2 sts, k2tog.

Rows 14 and 16: As row 12 (5 sts).

Row 18: K2tog, k1, k2tog (3 sts).

Row 19: K3tog and fasten off.

TO FINISH

Work in ends on all pieces. Sew seam of hat, matching stripes as you go. Fold hat in half with center seam at the back. Using a large crochet hook pull the antenna through the fabric on top of the hat, secure in the center. Roll each end of the antenna into a tight ball and sew firmly.

Fold mittens in half lengthwise, sew side seam matching stripes. Take a pair of wings and stitch together in the center, over lapping them slightly. Sew very firmly to the back of the mitten. Repeat with the other pair of wings.

Make 2 twisted cords about 13½ in (34 cm) long with black yarn (see page 20). Thread through the mittens at just about the second black stripe. Gather up and tie in a bow.

doggie slippers

Using shades of pale green yarn, knit these cute little doggie slippers in just an evening. The slippers are completed with tiny little dogs' heads, made separately and firmly sewn on afterwards.

♥ Beginner

MEASUREMENTS
To fit 3–6 month old baby

MATERIALS
- Sirdar Tiny Tots DK 90% acrylic/10% polyester (50 g balls; 150 yd/137 m): 1 x 50 g ball shade 925 Smoothie (A)
- Sirdar Snuggly DK (50 g balls; 179 yd/165 m): 1 x 50 g ball shade 403 Wobble (B)
- Oddments of cream, brown and black for dogs' heads
- Knitting needles size US 5 (UK 9/3¾ mm)
- Knitting needles size US 3 (UK 10/3¼ mm)
- Small amount of toy stuffing

GAUGE
22 sts x 30 rows measures 4 in (10 cm) square over st st using US 5 (UK 9/3¾ mm) needles

SPECIAL ABBREVIATIONS
M1 = make a stitch by pick up strand of yarn between stitches and knitting into back of it

SLIPPERS
Make two alike.
Using US 5 (UK 9/3¾ mm) needles and yarn A cast on 27 sts.
Knit 1 row. Work shaping as follows:
Row 1: K2, (M1, k11, M1, k1) twice, k1 (31 sts).
Row 2: Knit.
Row 3: K2, M1, k12, M1, k3, M1, k12, M1, k2 (35 sts).
Row 4: Knit.
Row 5: K2, M1, k13, M1, K5, M1, k13, M1, k2 (39 sts).
Row 6: Knit.
Row 7: K2, M1, k14, M1, k7, M1, k14, M1, k2 (43 sts).
Row 8: Knit.
Join in yarn B and work picot edging:
Next row: Beg knit work 4 rows st st.
Next row: K1, *yf, k2tog*, rep from * to * to end of row.
Next row: Purl.
Work 2 more rows in st st. Break yarn B. Change to yarn A and work 12 rows in garter stitch.
Shape instep
Row 1: K26, turn.
Row 2: K9, turn.
Row 3: K8, k2tog, turn.
Row 4: K8, k2tog tbl, turn.
Rep last 2 rows 5 times more.
Next row: K9, then knit across remaining sts on

left-hand needle.

Next row: Knit across all stitches, decreasing 1 st in center of row (30 sts).

Now knit 2 rows in garter stitch across all stitches. Change to yarn B and work in k2, p2 rib for 23 rows. Change to yarn A and work 2 rows in k2, p2 rib. Bind off loosely in rib.

DOG'S HEAD
Make two alike.

Using US 3 (UK 10/3¼ mm) needles and cream yarn cast on 4 sts. Purl 1 row.

Next row (RS): Inc in each st to end (8 sts).

Next row: Purl.

Next row: Inc in each st to end (16 sts).

Next row: Purl.

Work 6 rows in st st.

Next row: (K2tog) 8 times (8 sts).

Next row: Purl.

Next row: (K2tog) 4 times (4 sts).

Next row: Purl.

Do not bind off. Run thread through remaining stitches, draw up tight and secure. Stitch seam but add stuffing as you do. Close seam. Take a blunt-ended needle and thread yarn through every stitch on the 6th row of st st before the dec row. Draw up quite firmly to form the muzzle of the dog. Fasten off.

Ears
Make four alike.

Using US 3 (UK 10/3¼ mm) needles and brown yarn cast on 2 sts.

Knit 1 row.

Next row: Inc in each st (4 sts).

Next row: Knit.

Next row: Inc in first st, k2, inc in last st (6 sts).

Now work 4 rows in garter stitch.

Next row: K2tog, k2, k2tog (4 sts).

Next row: (K2tog) twice (2 sts).

Next row: K2tog and bind off.

TO FINISH
Work in all ends. Working from wrong side of piece fold picot edging together, sew the first and last rows in yarn B knitting together, matching stitch for stitch. This will form the pointed picot edge on the right side of the slipper. Sew slipper foot and back seams. Fold over ribbed top in half to form cuff.

To complete dog's head, sew ears to either side of the head as shown in photograph. Using black yarn embroider nose, eyes and mouth. Use photograph as a guide if needed. Stitch heads very firmly to fronts of both slippers.

lemon sherbet sweater

A pretty flower motif decorates the front of this delightful sweater for tiny babies. Frilled edges on the bottom and around the sleeves make it extra special. The sweater is worked mainly in reverse stockinette stitch.

♥♥♥ Experienced

MEASUREMENTS
To fit newborn–3 month old baby. Chest 18 in (46 cm); length 10 in (25 cm); sleeve length 6 in (15 cm).

MATERIALS
- Sirdar Snuggly Kisses DK, 45% acrylic/55% nylon (50 g balls: 179 yd/165 m): 3 x 50 g balls shade 760 Sunshine
- Knitting needles size US 5 (UK 9/3¾ mm)
- Knitting needles size US 3 (UK 10/3¼ mm)
- Crochet hook size US E4 (UK 9/3½ mm)
- Cable needle
- Stitch markers
- 3 x small matching buttons.

GAUGE
- 22 sts x 30 rows measures 4 in (10 cm) square over reverse st st using US 5 (UK 9/3¾ mm) needles

SPECIAL ABBREVIATIONS
MB = make bobble as follows: K1, p1, k1, p1 into st, turn, p4, turn, lift 3 of 4 sts just made over first st, then knit into back of this st.
TW3F (worked over next 3 sts) = slip next st onto cable needle and leave at front of work, purl next 2 sts, knit st from cable needle, slip all stitches off together.

PB1 (worked over next 2 sts) = purl into back of 2nd st, knit next st, slip sts off needle together.
KF1 (worked over next 2 sts) = knit into front of 2nd st, purl next st, slip sts off needle together.

Note: the large number of stitches that are cast on will be decreased over the 12-row border pattern.

Pattern panel for flower motif worked over 15 sts
Row 1: P6, k1, p1, k1, p6.
Row 2: K5, p2, k1, p2, k5.
Row 3: P4, k2tog, k1, yfrn, p1, yo, k1, k2tog, p4.
Row 4: K4, p3, k1, p3, k4.
Row 5: P3, k2tog, k1, yf, k1, p1, k1, yf, k1, k2tog tbl, p3.
Row 6: K3, p4, k1, p4, k3.
Row 7: P2, k2tog, k1, yf, k2, p1, k2, yf, k1, k2tog tbl, p2.
Row 8: K2, p5, k1, p5, k2.
Row 9: P1, k2tog, k1, yf, k3, p1, k3, yf, k1, k2tog tbl, p1.
Row 10: K1, p6, k1, p6, k1.
Row 11: K2tog, k1, yf, k4, p1, k4, yf, k1, k2tog tbl.
Row 12: P7, k1, p7.

Row 13: K4, k2tog, k1, yf, k1, yf, k1, k2tog tbl, k4.
Row 14: P6, k1, p1, k1, p6.
Row 15: K3, k2tog, k1, yfrn, p1, k1, p1, yo, k1, k2tog tbl, k3.
Row 16: P5, k2, p1, k2, p5.
Row 17: K2, k2tog, k1, yfrn, p2, k1, p2, yo, k1, k2tog tbl, k2.
Row 18: P4, k3, p1, k3, p4.
Row 19: K1, k2tog, k1, yfrn, p2, MB, k1, MB, p2, yo, k1, k2tog tbl, k1.
Row 20: P3, k3, p1, k1, p1, k3, p3.
Row 21: K2tog, k1, yfrn, p1, MB, p5, MB, p1, yo, k1, k2tog tbl.
Row 22: P1, k13, p1.
Row 23: P3, MB, p7, MB, p3.
Row 24: K15.
Row 25: P3, MB, p7, MB, p3.
Row 26: K15.
Row 27: P4, MB, p5, MB, p4.
Row 28: Knit 15.
Row 29: P6, MB, p1, MB, p6.
Note: These 29 rows form pattern panel.

BACK

**Using US 5 (UK 9/3¾ mm) needles cast on 159 sts. Work border pattern as follows:
Row 1 (RS): P3, *k9, p3*, rep from * to * to end.
Row 2: K3, *p9, k3*, rep from * to * to end.
Row 3: P3, *yb, sl1, k1, psso, k5, k2tog, p3* rep from * to * to end.
Row 4: K3, *p7, k3* rep from * to * to end.
Row 5: P3, *yb, sl1, k1, psso, k3, k2tog, p3* rep from * to * to end.
Row 6: K3, *p5, k3*, rep from * to * to end.
Row 7: P3, *yb, sl1, k1, psso, k1, k2tog, P3*, rep from * to * to end.

Row 8: K3, *p3, k3*, rep from * to * to end.
Row 9: P3, *yb, sl1, k2tog, psso, p3*, rep from * to * to end (55 sts).
Row 10: K3, *p1, k3*, rep from * to * to end.
Row 11: P3, *k1, p3* rep from * to * to end.
Row 12: As row 10.
Row 13: As row 11.
Row 14: As row 10.
Row 15: P7, *k1, p3, k1, P7* rep from * to * to end.
Row 16: *K7, p1, k3, p1*, rep from * to * to last 7 sts, k7.
Row 17: P7, *PB1, p1, KF1, p7*, rep from * to * to end.
Row 18: K8, *p1, k1, p1, k9*, rep from * to * to last 11 sts, p1, k1, p1, k8.
Row 19: P8, *TW3F, p9*, rep from * to * to last 11 sts, TW3F, p8.
Row 20: K8, *p1, k11*, rep from * to * to last 11 sts, p1, k10.
These 20 rows complete border pattern.
Next row (RS): Purl.
Next row: Knit. **
Repeat last 2 rows until work measures 6 in (15 cm) ending on a knit row.

Shape raglans
Bind off 2 st at the beg of next 2 rows (51 sts).
Next row: K1, sl1, k1, psso, purl to last 3 sts, k2tog, k1.
Next row: K1, p1, knit to last 2 sts, p1, k1. Repeat last two rows until 19 sts remain, ending on a WS row. Leave stitches on a stitch holder.

FRONT

Work as for back from ** to **. Repeat last two rows 7 times more, ending on a knit row. Now place flower motif (use stitch markers either side of panel):
Row 1: Purl 20, pattern panel row 1, purl 20.
Row 2: Knit 20, pattern panel row 2, knit 20.

Continue working reverse st st either side of the pattern panel until work measures the same as back to armholes, ending on a WS row. Continue working pattern panel until all 29 rows have been completed then work these 15 st in reverse st st, at the same time shape raglans as for back until 33 sts remain, ending on a WS row.

Divide for neck

Next row: P1, sl1, k1, psso, k9, turn and leave rem sts on a spare needle.

Dec 1 st at neck edge on next 3 rows, at the same time, dec as before at raglan edge on following alt row (7 sts).

Dec at raglan edge only on next and following 4 alt rows (2 sts).

Work 1 row.

Next row: K2tog and fasten off. With RS facing, slip center 9 sts onto spare needle, work to last 3 sts, k2tog, p1. Work to match first side, reversing shapings.

SLEEVES

Make two alike.

Using US 5 (UK 9/3¾ mm) needles cast on 87 sts.
Work border pattern as follows:

Row 1 (RS): P3, *k9, p3*, rep from * to * to end.

Row 2: K3, *p9, k3*, rep from * to * to end.

Row 3: P3, *yb, sl1, k1, psso, k5, k2tog, p3* rep from
* to * to end.

Row 4: K3, *p7, k3*, rep from * to * to end.

Row 5: P3, *yb, sl1, k1, psso, k3, k2tog, p3*, rep from
* to * to end.

Row 6: K3, *p5, k3*, rep from * to * to end.

Row 7: P3, *yb, sl1, k1, psso, k1, k2tog, p3*, rep from
* to * to end

Row 8: K3, *p3, k3*, rep from * to * to end.

Row 9: P3, *yb, sl1, k2tog, psso, p3*, rep from
* to * to end (31 sts).

Row 10: K3, *p1, k3*, rep from * to * to end.

Row 11: P3, *k1, p3*, rep from * to * to end.

Row 12: As row 10.

Work 4 rows in reverse st st, ending with a knit row
and increasing 11 sts evenly on last row (42 sts).
Continue in reverse st st until work measures 6 in
(15 cm), ending on a WS row.

Shape raglans

Bind off 2 sts at beg of next 2 rows (38 sts).

Next row: K1, sl1, k1, psso, purl to last 3 sts, k2tog, k1.

Next row: K1, p1, knit to last 2 sts, p1, k1.

Repeat the last 2 rows until 6 sts remain, ending on a
WS row. Leave sts on a stitch holder.

NECK BAND

Join raglan seams leaving left back seam open.
With RS facing and using US 3 (UK 10/3¼ mm), knit
6 sts from left sleeve, pick up and knit 10 sts from
side of neck, knit 9 sts from center front, pick up and

knit 10 sts from other side of neck, knit 6 sts across
right sleeve and finally 19 sts from back (68 sts).
Work 7 rows in garter stitch on these sts. Bind off
firmly. Join remaining raglan seam for 1½ in (4 cm),
then join side and sleeve seams. Using US E4 (UK
9/3½ mm) crochet hook work a row of dc around
opening, making 3 button loops spaced along one
side. Sew on buttons to correspond with loops.

flowers and squares blanket

Delicate pastel colors combined with garter stitch and raised stockinette stitch squares are used to create this gorgeous snuggly baby blanket. Made in four strips of alternating colors this project is simple enough for the novice knitter to make.

♥ Beginner

MEASUREMENTS
23¹/₂ in (60 cm) x 29¹/₂ in (75 cm)

MATERIALS
- Sirdar Baby Supersoft Aran 100% Acrylic (100 g balls; 258yds/236 m): 1 x 100 g ball in each in the following shades: 831 Cream; 842 Pretty Pink; 885 Jellybabe; 880 Gingham Green
- Oddments of different shades for flowers
- Knitting needles US 8 (UK 6/size 5)

GAUGE
25 sts x 44 rows measures 6 in (15 cm) square over st st
1 square measures 6 in (15 cm) square

Note: The blanket is made in four strips, each strip having 5 squares of alternating garter stitch and st st raised pattern.

BASIC STRIP

Using US 8 (UK 6/5 mm) needles and specified color cast on 25 sts.
Square 1: Work 44 rows in garter stitch.
Change color and proceed to second square.
Square 2: Work 8 rows in garter stitch.
Work raised pattern:
Row 1: Knit.
Row 2: K5, purl 15, k5.
Repeat last 2 rows 13 times more.
Now work 8 rows garter stitch over all stitches.
Square 3: Change color and work as Square 1.
Square 4: Change color and work as Square 2.
Square 5: Change color and work as Square 1.

The color sequence for the blanket is as follows:
Strip A: Jellybabe, Cream, Pretty Pink, Gingham Green, Jellybabe.
Strip B: Cream, Gingham Green, Jellybabe, Pretty Pink, Cream.
Strip C: Gingham Green, Pretty Pink, Cream, Jellybabe, Gingham Green.
Strip D: Pretty Pink, Jellybabe, Gingham Green, Cream, Pretty Pink

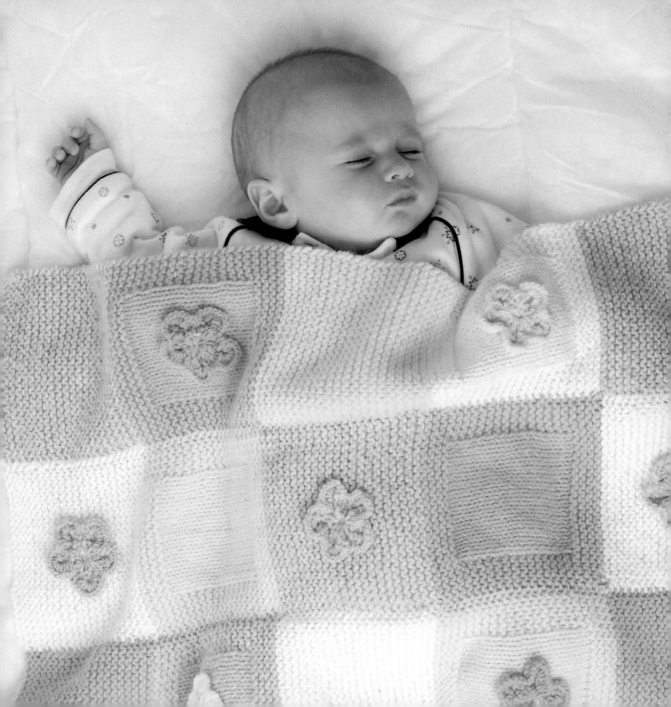

FLOWERS

Make 10 in various colors.

Using US 8 (UK 6/5 mm) needles and color of your choice cast on 57 sts.

Row 1: Purl.

Row 2: K2, *k1, slip this st back onto left-hand needle, lift the next 8 sts on left-hand needle over this st and off the needle, yo twice, knit the first st again, k2*, rep from * to * to end.

Row 3: K1, *p2tog, drop loop of 2 sts made in previous row and (k1, k1 tbl) into loop, p1*, rep from * to * to last st, k1. Do not bind off, break yarn and run thread through stitches, draw up into a flower shape and secure, sew side seams.

TO FINISH

Work in ends neatly on all pieces.

Set blanket out in four strips lettered A, B, C, D, with A being on the right hand side and the other strips following in sequence.

Join the strips together using a flat seam and matching yarn, on the right side of the work by picking up the little "bumps" of the garter stitch on adjacent sides of the squares and drawing them together firmly. This gives an almost invisible seam. It takes a little practice to get this right so be patient.

Work in ends on flowers, stitch to alternate squares on blanket using the photographs as a guide.

sweet pea cardigan and hat

Delicate shades of pink in a super-soft random dyed yarn are used to create this gorgeous top and matching hat. Reverse stockinette stitch is used in the main part of the cardigan while an unusual frilled edge makes it a little bit special.

♥♥♥ Experienced

MEASUREMENTS
To fit newborn–3 month old baby.
Chest 18 in (46 cm);
length 10 in (26 cm); sleeve length 2 in (5 cm)

MATERIALS
- Sirdar Snuggly Kisses DK acrylic 45%/55% nylon (50 g balls; 179 yd/165 m): 3 x 50 g balls shade 758 Princess Pink
- 1 yd/1 m narrow matching satin ribbon
- 5 x small pink heart buttons.
- Knitting needles size US 5 (UK 9/3¾ mm)
- Knitting needles size US 3 (UK10/3¼ mm)
- Crochet hook size US E4 (UK 9/3½ mm)

GAUGE
22 sts x 30 rows measures 4 in (10 cm) square over reverse st st using US 5 (UK 9/3¾ mm) needles

Note: the large number of stitches that are cast on will be decreased over the 12-row border pattern.

BACK
Using US 5 (UK 9/3¾ mm) needles cast on 159 sts.
Work border pattern as follows:
Row 1 (RS): P3, *k9, p3*, rep from * to * to end.
Row 2: K3, *p9, k3*, rep from * to * to end.
Row 3: P3, *yb, sl1, k1, psso, k5, k2tog, p3*, rep from * to * to end.
Row 4: K3, *p7, k3*, rep from * to * to end.
Row 5: P3, *yb, sl1, k1, psso, k3, k2tog, p3*, rep from * to * to end.
Row 6: K3, *p5, k3*, rep from * to * to end.
Row 7: P3, *yb, sl1, k1, psso, k1, k2tog, p3* rep from * to * to end.
Row 8: K3, *p3, k3*, rep from * to * to end.
Row 9: P3, *yb, sl1, k2tog, psso, p3*, rep from * to * to end (55 sts).
Row 10: K3, *p1, k3*, rep from * to * to end.
Row 11: P3, *k1, p3*, rep from * to * to end.
Row 12: As row 10.
Now work in reverse st st as follows:
Row 1 (RS): Purl.
Row 2: Knit.
Continue in reverse st st until work measures 6 in (15 cm), ending on a knit row.
Shape raglans
Bind off 2 at beginning of the next 2 rows (51 sts).
Next row: K1, sl1, k1, psso, purl to last 3 sts, k2tog, k1.

Next row: K1, p1, knit to last 2 sts, p1, k1.
Repeat last 2 rows until 19 sts remain, ending on a WS row. Leave sts on a stitch holder.

LEFT FRONT
**Using US 5 (UK 9/3¾ mm) needles cast on 75 sts.
Work border pattern as follows:
Row 1 (RS): P3, *k9, p3*, rep from * to * to end.
Row 2: K3, *p9, k3*, rep from * to * to end.
Row 3: P3, *yb, sl1, k1, psso, k5, k2tog, p3*, rep from * to * to end.
Row 4: K3, *p7, k3*, rep from * to * to end.
Row 5: P3, *yb, sl1, k1, psso, k3, k2tog, p3*, rep from * to * to end.
Row 6: K3, *p5, k3*, rep from * to * to end.
Row 7: P3, *yb, sl1, k1, psso, k1, k2tog, p3*, rep from * to * to end.
Row 8: K3, *p3, k3*, rep from * to * to end.
Row 9: P3, *yb, sl1, k2tog, psso, p3*, rep from * to * to end.
Row 10: K3, *p1, k3*, rep from * to * to end.
Row 11: P3, *k1, p3*, rep from * to * to end.
Row 12: As row 10.
Continue in reverse st st until front measures same as back to beg of raglan shaping, ending on a WS row. **
Shape raglans
Bind off 2 st at beg of next row (25 sts).
Knit 1 row.
Next row: K1, sl1, k1, psso, purl to end.
Next row: Knit to last 2 sts, p1, k1.
Rep last 2 rows until 16 sts remain, ending on RS row.
Shape neck
Next row: Bind off 4 sts, knit to last 2 sts, p1, k1.
Continue to dec 1 st at raglan edge as before and at the same time dec 1 st at neck edge on the next and 2 following alt rows (6 sts).

Dec 1 st at raglan edge only on every following alt row until 2 sts remain, ending on a WS row.
Next row: Sl1, k1, psso, and fasten off.

RIGHT FRONT
Work as left front from ** to ** BUT end on a RS row.
Shape raglan
Bind off 2 sts at beg of next row (25 sts).
Next row: Purl to last 3 sts, k2tog, k1.
Next row: K1, p1, knit to end.
Now continue as for left front but reversing neck shapings and working k2tog in place of sl1, k1, psso.

SLEEVES
Make two alike.
Using US 5 (UK 9/3¾ mm) needles cast on 42 sts.
Work 3 rows in garter stitch.
Work 4 rows in reverse st st.
Next row: K2, *yf, k2tog, k1*, rep from * to * to last st, k1.
Work 5 rows in reverse st st, ending on a WS row.
Shape raglans
Bind off 2 sts at beg of next 2 rows (38 sts).
Next row: K1, sl1, k1, psso, purl to last 3 sts, k2tog, k1.
Next row: K1, p1, knit to last 2 sts, p1, k1.
Repeat last 2 rows until 6 sts remain, ending on a WS row. Leave sts on a stitch holder.
Join raglan seams on front, sleeves and back.

RIGHT FRONT BAND
With RS facing and US 3 (UK 10/3¼ mm) needles, pick up and knit 64 sts evenly along right front, working from base to neck and beginning just above the border pattern.
Work 3 rows in garter stitch.

Buttonhole row: Knit 4, (yf, k2tog, k14) 3 times, yf, k2tog, k10.
Work 2 rows in garter stitch. Bind off firmly.

LEFT FRONT BAND
Work as right front band but start at neck edge when picking up the stitches and omit the buttonholes.

NECKBAND
With RS facing and US 3 (UK 10/3¼ mm) needles, pick up and knit 5 sts along top of right front band, 10 sts up side of neck, knit 6 sts from right sleeve, 19 sts from back, 6 sts from left sleeve, pick up and knit 10 sts down other side of neck and then 5 sts from left front band (61 sts).
Work 3 rows in garter stitch.
Next row: K3, yf, k2tog, knit to end.
Work 4 more rows in garter stitch.
Bind off firmly.

HAT

Using US 5 (UK 9/3¾ mm) needles cast on 84 sts.
Work 6 rows in garter stitch.
Work 26 rows in reverse st st.
Now proceed to shape the top as follows:
Row 1: K3, (k2tog, k4) 13 times, k2tog, k1 (70 sts).
Row 2: Purl.
Row 3: K2, (k2tog, k3) 13 times, k2tog, k1 (56 sts).
Row 4: Purl.
Row 5: K1, (k2tog, k2) 13 times, k2tog, k1 (42 sts).
Row 6: Purl.
Row 7: (K2tog, k1) 14 times (28 sts).
Row 8: Purl.
Row 9: (K2tog) 14 times (14 sts).
Break yarn and run through remaining sts, draw up
tight and secure.

CROCHET FLOWERS

Make two alike.
**Using US E4 (UK 9/3½ mm) crochet hook make
6 ch, join with a sl st into a circle.
Next round: (6ch, 1sc into circle) 6 times
(6 petals).**
Next round: Sl st into first 6 ch sp, 3ch, 3dc into
same 6 ch sp, sl st into next sc, (4dc into 6 ch sp, sl st
into next sc) 5 times. Fasten off.

Small flowers

Make two alike.
Work as for large flower from ** to **. Fasten off.

TO FINISH

Work in any ends neatly on all pieces. Sew side and
sleeve seams on cardigan. Sew two flowers, 1 large
and 1 small onto front of cardigan as shown in
photograph. Sew on buttons to correspond with
button holes. Cut ribbon into two equal lengths,
thread through holes on sleeves, tie into a neat bow.
  Sew back seam on hat. Fold hat in half with seam
at center back. Attach flowers, 1 large and 1 small to
one side of the hat.

Edward Bear

No nursery is complete without the addition of a cuddly teddy. This charming little fellow is made of a soft bamboo blend yarn and is a perfect gift for even the smallest baby. I've used cream and brown but choose colors to suit your own taste.

♥♥ Intermediate

• •

MEASUREMENTS
Edward Bear is approximately 12 in (30 cm) tall

MATERIALS
- Sirdar Snuggly Baby Bamboo DK 80% Bamboo/20% Wool (50 g balls; 104 yd/95 m): 3 x 50 g balls shade 131 Cream (A); 1 x 50 g ball shade 128 Tigger (B); Oddment of shade 153 Jelly Baby (C)
- Small amount of black yarn for embroidery
- Knitting needles size US 5 (UK 9/3¾ mm)
- Fiberfill stuffing

GAUGE
Gauge is not critical with this project.

Note: Worked in garter stitch throughout.

• •

HEAD
Using US 5 (UK 9/3¾ mm) needles and yarn A cast on 40 sts.
Knit 4 rows.
Dec 1 st at each end of next row and every following 3rd row until 4 sts remain.
Next row: (K2tog) twice.
Next row: K2tog and fasten off.

Muzzle
Using US 5 (UK 9/3¾ mm) needles and yarn B cast on 10 sts.
Knit 1 row.
Inc 1 st at each end of next 2 rows (14 sts).
Cast on 2 sts at beg of next 2 rows (18 sts).
Knit 6 rows.
Bind off 2 sts at beg of next 2 rows (14 sts).
Dec 1 st at each end of next 3 rows (8 sts).
Knit 2 rows. Bind off.

BODY
Make two alike.
Using US 5 (UK 9/3¾ mm) needles and yarn A cast on 10 sts.
Knit 4 rows.
Inc 1 st at each end of next and every following alt row until there are 24 sts.

Knit 36 rows.
Dec 1 st at each end of next and every following alt row until 14 sts remain. Bind off (this is neck edge).

ARMS

Make two alike.
Using US 5 (UK 9/3¾ mm) needles and yarn A cast on 8 sts.
Knit 1 row.
Next row: Inc in every st (16 sts).

Knit 2 rows.
Inc 1 st at each end of next and every following alt row until there are 24 sts.
Knit 20 rows.
Decrease for top of arm.
Next row: K2tog at each end of row.
Next row: Knit.
Repeat last two rows once more. Bind off.

LEGS

Make two alike.
Using US 5 (UK 9/3¾ mm) needles and yarn A cast on 16 sts.
Knit 1 row.
Next row: Inc in every st (32 sts).
Knit 2 rows.
Next row: K12, (k2tog) 4 times, k12 (28 sts).
Knit 26 rows.
Dec 1 st at each end of next row (26 sts).
Knit 1 row.
Next row: (K2tog) 13 times (13 sts). Bind off.

ARM PADS

Make two alike.
Using US 5 (UK 9/3¾ mm) needles and yarn B cast on 8 sts.
Knit 4 rows.
Dec 1 st at each end of next and following alt row (4 sts). Bind off.

FOOT PADS

Make two alike.
Using US 5 (UK 9/3¾ mm) needles and yarn B cast on 4 sts.
Knit 2 rows.

Inc 1 st at each end of next and every following alt row until there are 10 sts.
Knit 2 rows.
Dec 1 st at each end of next row and every following alt rows until 4 sts remain. Bind off.

EARS

Make two alike.
Using US 5 (UK 9/3¾ mm) needles and yarn B cast on 8 sts.
Knit 1 row.
Inc 1 st at each end of next 5 rows (18 sts).
Knit 4 rows.
Next row: (K2tog) 9 times (9 sts). Bind off.

BOW

Using US 5 (UK 9/3¾ mm) needles and yarn C cast on 7 sts.
Row 1: Sl1, knit to end.
Repeat Row 1 until piece is long enough to go around the bear's neck and tie in a neat bow at the front.

TO FINISH

Work in all ends on pieces. Follow the diagrams below for finishing the bear's head. Stuff the head and get a nice shape. Attach the ears, one on either side, curling them slightly when stitching to give a curved shape. Take the muzzle and stitch it in place on the bear's head, stuff lightly to give a nice shape. Embroider eyes, nose and mouth with black yarn, using photograph as a guide.

Sew body sections together, leaving the neck edge open for stuffing. Stuff firmly and shape, then close the opening.

Sew up the arms, seams to be at center back, leaving the top open to stuff. Shape as you do, and after stuffing, sew closed. Sew a paw pad to each arm, using photo as guide. Sew up the legs, seam at the center back as on arms. Leave top of leg open, stuff and shape, then sew up opening. Sew a foot pad in place on each leg. Now attach the arms and legs firmly to the body. The teddy is in a sitting position so attach the legs accordingly. Tie his bow on firmly and stitch in place.

Fold lines for bear's head

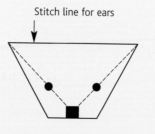

Stitch line for ears

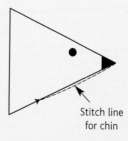

Stitch line for chin

berrylicious baby

Both time and patience will be required when making this delicious little outfit using soft pure wool in colors and patterning that resembles a strawberry. Take care not to pull the contrasting yarn too tightly, which could result in puckering.

♥♥♥ Experienced

MEASUREMENTS
To fit baby 6–12 months
Chest 20 in (51 cm); length 11 in (28 cm);
sleeve length 7 in (17.5 cm)

MATERIALS
- Rowan Pure Wool DK 100% Superwash wool
  (50 g balls: 137 yds/125 m, worsted weight):
  5 x 50 g balls shade 036 Kiss (C); 3 x 50 g balls shade
  020 Parsley (G); 1 x 50 g ball shade 043 Flour (W);
  2 x 50 g balls shade 032 Gilt (L)
- Knitting needles size US 5 (UK 9/3¾ mm)
- Knitting needles size US 6 (UK 8/4 mm)
- Crochet hook size, US E4 (UK 9/3½ mm)
- 6 x small buttons

GAUGE
22 sts x 30 rows measures 4 in (10 cm) square worked
over st st on US 6 (UK 8/4 mm) needles

SPECIAL ABBREVIATIONS
M1 = make a stitch by picking up the strand of yarn
between the stitches and knitting into the back of it.

CARDIGAN
Back
Using US 5 (UK 9/3¾ mm) needles and yarn G cast
on 60 sts.
Work 10 rows in k1, p1 rib. Break yarn G
Change to US 6 (UK 8/4 mm) needles and yarn C,
working in st st and joining in and breaking yarn L as
required, proceed as follows:
Using yarn C, work 6 rows in st st.
Work spot pattern as follows:
Next row (RS): K3 C, *k1 L, k5 C*, rep from * to * to
last 3 sts, k1 L, k2 C.
Using yarn C, work 5 rows in st st.
Next row: K6 C *k1 L, k5 C*, rep from * to * end.
Using yarn C, work 5 rows in st st.
The last 12 rows form the spot pattern repeat for
back.
Continue in spot pattern until work measures 6 in
(15 cm), ending on a WS row.
Shape armholes
Keeping pattern correct, bind off 4 sts at beg of next
2 rows (52 sts).
Work straight until armhole measures 5 in (13 cm),
ending on a purl row.
Shape shoulders
Bind off 8 sts at beg of next 4 rows (20 sts). Leave
these sts on a stitch holder for back neck.

Right front

Using US 5 (UK 9/3¾ mm) needles and yarn G cast on 36 sts.

Work 4 rows in k1, p1 rib.

Buttonhole row: Rib 2, yf, rib 2tog, rib to end.

Work 4 rows more in rib.

Next row: Rib to last 6 sts, turn and slip these 6 sts on to a safety pin for the front band (30 sts). Break yarn G.

Change to US 6 (UK 8/4 mm) needles and yarn C, working in st st and joining in and breaking off yarn L as required, proceed as follows:

Using yarn C, work 6 rows in st st.

Work spot pattern as follows:

Next row (RS): K2 C, *k1 L, k5 C*, rep from * to * to last 4 sts, k1 L, k3 C.

Using yarn C, work 5 rows in st st.

Next row: *K5 C, k1 L*, rep from * to * to last 6 sts, k6 C.

Using yarn C, work 5 rows in st st.

The last 12 rows from the spot pattern repeat for right front. Continue in spot pattern until right front matches back to armhole, ending on a RS row.

Shape armhole

Keeping pattern correct, bind off 4 sts at beg of next row (26 sts).

Work straight until 11 rows less than on back have been worked before shoulder shaping, ending on a purl row.

Shape neck

Bind off 4 sts at beg of next row (22 sts).

Dec 1 st at neck edge on next 4 rows, then on 2 following alt rows (16 sts).

Work 2 rows without shaping, ending on a knit row

Shape shoulder

Bind off 8 sts at beg of next row. Work 1 row. Bind off remaining 8 sts.

Left front

Using US 5 (UK 9/3¾ mm) needles and yarn G cast on 36 sts. Work 9 rows in k1, p1 rib.

Next row: Rib 6 sts, slip these 6 sts onto a safety pin for front band, rib to end (30 sts). Break yarn.

Change to US 6 (UK 8/4 mm) needles and yarn C, working in st st and joining in and breaking off yarn L as required, proceed as follows:

Using yarn C, work 6 rows in st st.

Work spot pattern as follows:

Next row (RS): K3 C, *k1 L, k5 C*, rep from * to * to last 3 sts, k1 L, k2 C.

Using yarn C, work 5 rows in st st.

Next row: K6 C, *k1 L, k5 C*, repeat from * to * to end.

Using yarn C, work 5 rows in st st.

The last 12 rows form the spot pattern repeat for left front.

Continue in spot pattern until left front matches back to armhole, ending on a WS row.

Work to match right front, reversing all shapings.

Sleeves

Make two alike.

Using US 5 (UK 9/3¾ mm) needles and yarn G cast on 38 sts.

Work 10 rows in k1, p1 rib. Break yarn G.

Change to US 6 (UK 8/4 mm) needles and yarn C and work 6 rows in st st, inc 1 st at each end of 5th row (40 sts).

Join in yarn L and set the first row of spot pattern as follows:

Next row (RS): K4 C, *k1 L, k5 C*, rep from * to * to end.

Keeping spot pattern correct as worked before continue to shape sleeve by inc 1 st at each end of 2nd and every following 4th row until there are 58 sts. Continue in spot pattern until work measures 7 in (17.5 cm), ending on a purl row. Bind off loosely.

Left front band

Using US 5 (UK 9/3¾ mm) needles and yarn G, rejoin yarn to stitches on safety pin, continue in k1, p1 rib until band, when slightly stretched, fits up left front to beginning of neck shaping. Break yarn and leave sts on a safety pin.

Right front band

Work as left front band with addition of 5 more buttonholes evenly spaced along the band. Break yarn and leave sts on safety pin.

Neck band

Join shoulder seams of back and fronts.
With RS facing and using US 5 (UK 9/3¾ mm) needles and yarn G, rib across 6 sts from right front band, pick up and knit 16 sts up right side of neck, knit across 20 sts of back neck, pick up and knit 16 sts from left side of neck, then rib across 6 sts of left front band (64 sts).
Work 2 rows in k1, p1 rib.
Next row: Bind off 6 sts at the beg of the next 2 rows (52 sts).
Work 8 rows in rib over the remaining sts. Bind off loosely in rib.

FLOWERS AND LEAVES

Large flower

Make two alike.
** Using US E4 (UK 9/3½ mm) crochet hook and yarn W make 4 ch, join into a circle with a sl st.
Next round: (5ch, 1sc into circle), 5 times, join with a sl st. **
Next round: (1sc, 5dc,1sc, all into next 5ch loop) 5 times, join with a sl st to first sc. Fasten off.

Small flower

Make two alike.
Work as for large flower from ** to **. Fasten off.

Center for large flowers

Using same crochet hook and yarn L make 3ch, work 8dc into 2nd ch from hook, join with a sl st to form a circle. Fasten off and thread the loose end through the dcs, gather up to form a small ball, secure.

Center for small flowers

Work as for large flower center but work 8sc into 2nd ch from hook instead of 8dc.

Leaf

Using US 5 (UK 9/3¾ mm) needles and yarn G cast on 3 sts.

Knit 1 row.

Next row: K1, M1, p1, M1, k1 (5 sts).

Next row: Knit.

Next row: K2, M1, p1, M1, k2 (7 sts).

Next row: Knit.

Next row: K3, p1, k3.

Repeat last 2 rows twice more.

Next row: K2tog, k3, k2tog (5 sts).

Next row: K2, p1, k2.

Next row: K2tog, k1, k2tog (3 sts).

Next row: K3tog and fasten off.

HAT

Using US 5 (UK 9/3¾ mm) needles and yarn G cast on 92 sts.

Work 7 rows in k1, p1 rib.

Increase row: Rib 3, inc in next st, (rib 2, inc in next st) 28 times, rib 4 (121 sts). Break yarn G.

Change to US 6 (UK 8/4 mm) needles and yarn C, and work 6 rows in st st.

Join in yarn L and work in spot pattern as follows:

Next row (RS): K3 C, *k1 L, k5 C*, rep from * to * to last 4 sts, k1 L, k3 C.

Using yarn C, work 5 rows in st st.

Next row: K6 C, *k1 L, k5 C*, rep from * to * last 7 sts, k1 L, k6 C.

Using yarn C, work 5 rows in st st.

Next row: K3 C, *k1 L, k5 C*, rep from * to * to last 4 sts, k1 L, k3 C. Break yarn L. Continue in yarn C only

and work 3 rows in st st, ending on a purl row.

Shape crown as follows:

Row 1: K2, (k2tog, k7) 13 times, k2tog (107 sts).

Work 3 rows in st st.

Row 5: K2, (k2tog, k6) 12 times, k2tog, k7 (94 sts).

Work 3 rows in st st.

Row 9: K2, (k2tog, k5) 12 times, k2tog, k6 (81 sts).

Work 3 rows in st st.

Row 13: K2, (k2tog, k4) 12 times, k2tog, k5 (68 sts).

Work 3 rows in st st.

Row 17: K2, (k2tog, k3) 12 times, k2tog, k4 (55 sts).

Row 18: Purl.

Row 19: K2, (k2tog, k2) 12 times, k2tog, k3 (42 sts).

Row 20: Purl.

Row 21: K2, (k2tog, k1) 12 times, k2tog, k2 (29 sts).

Row 22: Purl.

Row 23: K2, (k2tog) across row to last st, k1 (16 sts).

Row 24: (P2tog) 8 times (8 sts).

Run yarn through remaining stitches, draw tight, secure and fasten off.

SOCKS

Make two alike.

Using US 5 (UK 9/3¾ mm) needles and yarn G cast on 27 sts. Work in k1, p1 rib for 4 in (10 cm).

Break yarn G and join in yarn C.

Working in st st and joining in yarn L as required, set spot pattern as follows:

Using yarn C, work 6 rows in st st.

Next row: K4 C, *k1 L, k5 C*, rep from * to * to last 5 sts, k1 L, k4 C.

Using yarn C, work 5 rows in st st.

Next row: K1 C, *k1 L, k5 C*, rep from * to * to last 2 sts, k1 L, k1 C.

Using yarn C, work 5 rows in st st.

Next row: K4 C, *k1 L, k5 C*, rep form * to * to last 5 sts, k1 L, k4 C.

Next row: Using yarn C, purl.

Shape heel using yarn C only as follows:

Next row: K3, turn.

Next row: Sl1, purl to end.

Next row: K5, turn.

Next row: Sl1, purl to end.

Next row: K3, turn.

Next row: Sl1, purl to end.

Next row: Knit to end.

Work other side to match reading purl for knit and knit for purl.

Keeping spot pattern correct across all sts continue until work measures 3½ in (8.5 cm) from last spot row, ending on a purl row.

Shape toe

Next row: K5, k2tog, k1, sl1, k1, psso, k7, k2tog, k1, sl1, k1, psso, k5 (23 sts).

Next row: Purl.

Next row: K4, k2tog, k1, sl1, k1, psso, k5, k2tog, k1, sl1, k1, psso, k4 (19 sts).

Next row: Purl.

Next row: K3, (k2tog, k1, sl1, k1, psso, k3) twice (15 sts).

Next row: Purl. Bind off

TO FINISH

Hat: Work in all ends. Join seam matching pattern. Sew flower and leaf to center of the hat.

Socks: Work in all ends. Join side and foot seams. Turn back cuff at top of sock.

Cardigan: Work in all ends. Sew sleeves into armholes, then join side and sleeve seams. Sew front bands in position on to fronts. Sew on buttons to correspond with buttonholes. Fold over neckband onto wrong side of work, sew in place but don't close ends. Make a chain or twisted cord 24 in (61 cm) long (see page 20). Thread through neckband, sew a small flower to each end of chain. Sew centers to flowers. Sew flower and two leaves to right front as shown in photograph.

baby blue booties

The softest baby yarn is used for these pretty booties. Worked mostly in garter stitch they are simple and quick to make. I've chosen blue but you can chose any color you like, then add contrasting ribbons and buttons to personalize them.

♥♥ Intermediate

MEASUREMENTS
To fit newborn–3 month old baby

MATERIALS
- Wendy Peter Pan Soft Blend 4ply, 55% nylon/45% acrylic (50 g balls; 225 yd/205 m): 1 x 50 g ball shade 306 Baby Blue
- Knitting needles size US 3 (UK 10/3¼ mm)
- 1 yd (1 m) narrow blue gingham check baby ribbon
- 2 x blue and white cat buttons (optional)

GAUGE
8 sts x 36 rows measures 4 in (10 cm) square over st st.

Note: Booties are worked entirely in garter stitch unless otherwise stated.

BOOTIES
Make two alike.
Using size US 3 (UK 10/3¼ mm) needles, cast on 36 sts.
Work 3 rows in garter stitch.
Next row: *K1, yf, k2tog*, rep from * to * to end.
Work 25 rows in garter stitch.
Next row: *K1, yf, k2tog*, repeat from * to * to end of row.
Next row: Knit.
Shape instep as follows:
Row 1: K24, turn.
Row 2: Sl1, K11, turn.
Repeat Row 2 for a further 20 rows. Break yarn.
With RS facing, rejoin yarn to sts on right-hand needle, pick up and knit 12 sts from first side of instep, knit across 12 sts of toe, pick up and knit 12 sts down other side of instep, knit across remaining sts on left hand needles (60 sts).
Work 10 rows in garter stitch.
Shape sole as follows:
Row 1: K2tog, k20, (k2tog) twice, k8, (k2tog) twice, k20, k2tog.
Row 2: K2tog, knit to last 2 sts, k2tog.

Row 3: K2tog, k17, (k2tog) twice. K6, (k2tog) twice, k17, k2tog.
Row 4: As row 2.
Row 5: K2tog, k14, (k2tog) twice, k4, (k2tog) twice, k14, k2tog.
Row 6: As row 2. Bind off remaining 36 sts.

TO FINISH

Work in ends and sew up the booties using a flat seam. Turn down cuff at the top of the booties, thread the ribbon through the holes at the ankle and tie in a bow. Sew a cat button very, very firmly onto the front of each bootie if you wish.

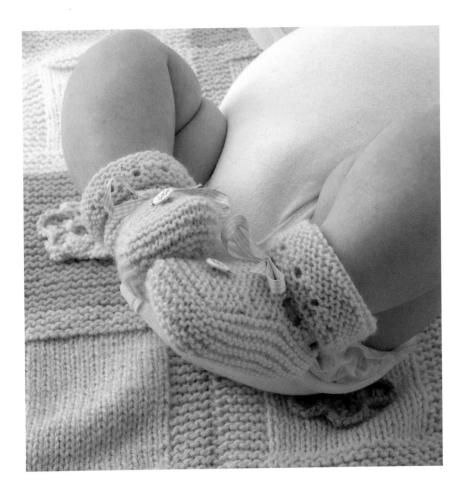

applique sleeping sack

Soft organic yarn is used to make this cozy sleeping sack. Knitted in stockinette stitch with a neat twisted rib on welts, front borders and around the snug-fitting hood, its brightly colored motifs are knitted separately and sewn on afterwards.

♥♥ Intermediate

MEASUREMENTS
To fit newborn–6 month old baby
Chest 22 in (56 cm); length from shoulders 23$\frac{1}{2}$ in (60 cm); sleeve length 8 in (20 cm)

MATERIALS
- Rowan Pure Life Organic Cotton, 100% organic cotton (50 g balls; 131 yd/120 m): 10 x 50 g balls in shade 986 Natural
- Oddments of DK yarn in red, green, yellow, black, white and turquoise for the motifs
- Knitting needles size US 3 (UK 10/3$\frac{1}{4}$ mm)
- Knitting needles size US 5 (UK 9/3$\frac{3}{4}$ mm)
- Knitting needles size US 6 (UK 8/4 mm)
- Crochet hook size US E4 (UK 9/3$\frac{1}{2}$ mm)
- Ready-made bows for the kite tail.
- 10 x matching buttons

GAUGE
24 sts x 32 rows measures 4 in (10 cm) square over st st

SPECIAL ABBREVIATIONS
TW2F = twist 2 front (worked over 2 stitches), knit into front of second stitch, do not slip stitch off needle, now knit into front of first stitch, slip both stitches off together.

SLEEPING SACK
Right front
Using US 6 (UK 8/4 mm) needles and main yarn cast on 50 sts.
Work twisted rib pattern as follows:
Row 1 (WS): K2, *p2, k2* rep from * to * to end.
Row 2: K1, p1, *TW2F, p2*, rep from * to * to last 4 sts, TW2F, p1, k1.
These 2 rows form the twisted rib pattern.
Work 9 more rows, ending on a WS row.
Change to st st with twisted rib panel for front border on last 10 sts as follows:
Row 1: K1, p1, (TW2F, p2) twice, knit to end.
Row 2: Purl to last 10 sts (k2, p2) twice, k2.
Work 18 rows more as set.
Shape sides by decreasing 1 st at side edge on next and following 10th rows (45 sts).
Continue as set until work measures 18$\frac{1}{2}$ in (47 cm), ending on a RS row.
Shape armholes
Keeping twisted rib panel correct, bind off 4 sts at beg of next row by binding off 4 sts at the beg of next row.
Dec 1 st at armhole edge on next and every following alt row until 34 sts remain.
Work straight until front measures 22 in (56 cm), ending at front edge.

Shape neck

Bind off 17 sts firmly at beg of next row (17 sts).
Dec 1 st at neck edge on every following alt row until 13 sts remain.
Work a few rows straight until front measures 23 in (59 cm), ending at armhole edge.

Shape shoulders

Bind off 7 sts at beg of next row.
Work 1 row. Bind off remaining 6 sts.

Left front

First mark position for 6 buttons on right front band, the first one to come 1 in (2 cm) from the bottom, and the last one to come 1 in (2 cm) below top of front band, then space the other four evenly along the band.
Work as for right front, reverse all shapings and working buttonholes to correspond with markers on right front.
Note: Work buttonhole as follows. Knit to last 10 sts, p2, TW2F, yrn, p2tog, TW2F, p1, K1.

Back

Using US 6 (UK 8/4 mm) needles and main yarn cast on 84 sts.
Work twisted rib pattern for bottom flap as follows.
Row 1 (WS): K3, *p2, k2*, rep from * to * to last st, k1.
Row 2: K1, p2, *TW2F, p2*, rep from * to * to last st, k1.
These two rows form the twisted rib pattern.
Work 3 more rows in twisted rib pattern
Buttonhole row: Pattern 9 sts, yrn, p2tog, (pattern 14 sts, yrn, p2tog) 4 times, pattern 9 sts.
Work 3 more rows in twisted rib pattern, ending on a WS row.
Change to st st with twisted rib edges as follows:

Row 1: K1, (p2, TW2F), twice, p1, knit to last 10 sts, p1, (TW2F, p2) twice, k1.
Work 26 rows more as set, ending on a WS row.
Starting with row 2, work in twisted rib as before for 8 rows, ending on a WS row.
Starting with a knit row, work in st st for 20 rows.
Row 2: K3, p2, k2, p2, k1, purl to last 10 sts, k1, p2, k2, p2, k3.
(Flap is completed).
Dec 1 st at each end of next row and 5 following 10th rows (72 sts). Continue straight until work measures 18½ in (47 cm), ending on a purl row.

Shape armholes

Bind off 4 sts at beg of next 2 rows (64 sts).
Dec 1 st at each end of next and every following alt row until 50 sts remain. Work straight until back matches fronts to start of shoulder shaping, ending on a purl row.

Shape shoulders

Bind off 7 sts at beg of next 2 rows, then 6 sts at beg of following 2 rows. Bind off remaining 24 sts.

Hood

With US 5 (UK 9/3¾ mm) needles and main yarn cast on 72 sts.
Work in twisted rib pattern as for back for 4 in (10 cm), ending on a RS row and increasing 5 sts evenly across last row (77 sts). (Pattern will now be reversed for turn-back on hood.)
Change to US 6 (UK 8/4 mm) needles and work in st st for 6 in (15 cm), ending on a purl row.
Bind off 6 sts at beg of next 10 rows. Bind off remaining 17 sts.

Sleeves

Make two alike.

Using US 3 (UK 10/3¼ mm) needles and main yarn cast on 34 sts.

Work in twisted rib pattern as follows:

Row 1 (WS): K1, p1, *k2, p2*, rep from * to * to last 4 sts, k2, p1, k1.

Row 2: (K2, *p2, TW2F*, rep from * to * to last 4 sts, p2, k2.

These two rows form twisted rib pattern.

Work 17 more rows in twisted rib pattern, inc 8 sts evenly across last row and ending on a WS row (42 sts).

Change to US 6 (UK 8/4 mm) needles and work in st st, shaping sides by inc 1 st at each end on the 9th and every following 4th row until there are 54 sts.

Continue on these sts until work measures 8 in (20 cm), ending on a purl row.

Shape top

Bind off 4 sts at beg of next two rows (46 sts).

Dec 1 st at each end of next and every following alt row until 32 sts remain.

Dec 1 st at each end of every row, until 22 sts remain. Bind off.

MOTIFS

Sun

Using US 5 (UK 9/3¾ mm) needles and yellow yarn cast on 7 sts.

Row 1: Purl.

Row 2: Inc in 1 st, knit to last st, inc in last st.

Row 3: Purl.

Repeat last 2 rows twice more (13 sts).

Work 4 rows st st.

Dec 1 st at each end of next and every following alt row until 7 sts remain. Bind off.

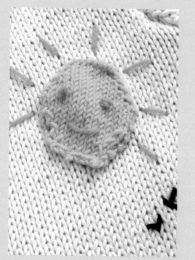

Kite

Using US 5 (UK 9/3¾ mm) needles and turquoise yarn cast on 3 sts.

Next row: Inc in first st, k1, inc in last st (5 sts).

Next row: Purl.

Inc 1 st at each end of next and every following alt row until there are 15 sts.

Work 5 rows in st st.

Dec 1 st at each end of every row until 3 sts remain.

Next row: K3tog and fasten off.

Tree

Using US 5 (UK 9/3¾ mm) needles and brown yarn cast on 7 sts.

Work in k1, p1 rib for 18 rows. Bind off.

Using same needles and green yarn cast on 10 sts.

Next row: Inc in first st, knit to last st, inc in last st.

Next row: Knit.

Repeat last 2 rows until there are 18 sts.

Knit 5 rows.

Next row: K2tog, knit to last 2 sts, k2tog.

Next row: Knit.

Repeat last 2 rows until 8 sts remain. Bind off.

Tractor

Body

Using US 5 needles and red yarn cast on 16 sts.

Work 12 rows in garter stitch.

Next row: Bind off 8 sts, knit to end.

Work 10 more rows in garter stitch. Bind off.

Large wheel

**Using US E4 (3½ mm) crochet hook and black yarn make 4ch, join into a circle with a sl st.

Round 1: 1ch, work 9sc into ring, sl st first sc.

Round 2: 1ch, work 2sc into each sc all around, sl st to first sc.**

Round 3: 1ch, (1sc into next sc, 2sc in next sc) 9 times, sl st to first sc.

Round 4: 1ch, work 1sc into each sc all around, sl st to first sc. Fasten off.

Small wheel

Work as large wheel from ** to **.

Wheel center (make two alike)

Using US E4 (3½ mm) crochet hook and pale yellow yarn make 4ch, join into a circle with a sl st.

Next round: 1ch, work 9sc into circle, sl st to first sc. Fasten off.

Smoke circles (make two alike)

Work as for wheel center.

Tractor chimney

Using US E4 (3½ mm) crochet hook and brown yarn make 6ch, work 1sc into 2nd ch from hook, 1sc into each, turn.

Next round: 1ch, 1sc into each sc to end. Fasten off.

TO FINISH

Join shoulder and side and sleeve seams with a fine backstitch. Set in sleeves. Sleeve border is folded in half and sewn double onto main part. Fold ribbing on hood in half onto right side of work and catch down. Join hood back seam. Pin hood in place around neck edge, beginning with inside front band on right front and ending at the same place on left front. Adjust to fit neatly as you pin, then stitch in place.

Sew on buttons to correspond with buttonholes. Fold up bottom flap and button onto main section. Center buttonhole on flap should button onto a button on front band.

Add motifs to front

Work in all ends on pieces. Using photograph as a guide place the pieces on to the front. Sew sun on carefully. Embroider eyes and a smiley mouth. Using straight stitches work sun's rays around the sun. Using black, embroider two birds just below the sun.

Sew centers of wheels to wheels. Place wheels on the body of the tractor, the larger wheel at the back. Sew in place. Tuck chimney behind the body and sew in place. Sew the tractor onto the front securely. Place smoke above tractor, sew in place.

Using black, embroider features on kite. Place on garment and pull into a nice diamond shape, and secure. Embroider tail of kite with turquoise yarn, now sew on three bows at random places along the tail as shown in photograph.

Take tree trunk and sew in place stretching out slightly at the base to give shape. Using red yarn embroider random French knots on to top of tree to represent apples. Now place treetop over trunk and sew in place.

shawl-collared jacket

Snuggle your little one into this pretty shawl-collared jacket. The yarn used has a slight slub giving a textured appearance to the knitting – I've used pale blue and white but there is a wonderful of range of shades to choose from in this yarn.

♥♥♥ Experienced

MEASUREMENTS
To fit 2–4 month old baby
Chest 18 in (46 cm); length from shoulder 11½ in (29 cm); sleeve length 7 in (17. 5 cm)

MATERIALS
- Sirdar Tiny Tots DK 90% acrylic/10% poly blend (50 g balls; 150 yd/137 m): 2 x 50 m balls shade 929 Hush (A); 2 x 50 m balls shade 932 Snug (B)
- Knitting needles size US 3 (UK 10/3¼ mm)
- Knitting needles size US 5 (UK 9/3¾ mm)
- 6 x matching buttons

GAUGE
22 st x 30 rows measures 4 in (10 cm) square over st st using US 5 (UK 9/3¾ mm) needles
Note: Carry yarns not in use loosely up the side of the work.

SPECIAL ABBREVIATIONS
PW = purlwise
YF = yarn to front of work
YB = yarn to back of work

BACK
Using US 3 (UK 10/3¼ mm) needles and yarn A cast on 58 sts.
Work in k2, p2 rib for 10 rows.
Change to US 5 (UK 9/3¾ mm) needles, join in yarn B and work pattern as follows:
Row 1 (RS): Using yarn B, knit.
Row 2: Using yarn B, purl.
Row 3: Using yarn A, k2, sl1 pw, *k3, sl1 pw*, rep from * to * to last 3 sts, k3.
Row 4: Using yarn A, k3, yf, sl 1 pw, yb, *k3, yf, sl1 pw, yb*, rep from * to * to last 2 sts, k2.
Row 5: Using yarn B, k4, *sl1 pw, k3*, rep from * to * to last 6 sts, sl1 pw, k5.
Row 6: Using yarn B, p5, *sl1 pw, p3*, rep from * to * to last 5 sts, sl1 pw, p4.
Row 7: Using yarn B, knit.
Row 8: Using yarn B, purl.
Row 9: Using yarn A, knit.
Row 10: Using yarn A, purl.
Row 11: Using yarn B, as row 3.
Row 12: Using yarn B, as row 4.
Row 13: Using yarn A, as row 5.
Row 14: Using yarn A, as row 6.
Row 15: Using yarn A, knit.
Row 16: Using yarn A, purl.

These 16 rows form the pattern and are repeated throughout. Continue in pattern for a further 16 rows, ending on a WS row.

Shape armholes
Keeping pattern correct dec 1 st at each end of next 4 rows (50 sts).
Work 22 rows straight in pattern, ending on a WS row.

Shape shoulders
Bind off 14 sts at beg of next 2 rows. Bind off remaining 22 sts.

LEFT FRONT
Using US 3 (UK 10/3¼ mm) needles and yarn A cast on 24 sts.
Work in k2, p2 rib for 10 rows.
Change to US 5 (UK 9/3¾ mm) needles, join in yarn B and work pattern as follows:
Row 1 (RS): Using yarn B, knit.
Row 2: Using yarn B, purl.
Row 3: Using yarn A, k3, *sl1, k3*, rep from * to * to last 5 sts, sl1, k4.
Row 4: Using yarn A, k4, *yf, sl1, yb, k3*, rep from * to * to end.
Row 5: Using yarn B, k5, *sl1 pw, k3*, rep from * to * to last 3 sts, sl1 pw, k2.
Row 6: Using yarn B, p2, *sl1 pw, p3*, rep from * to * to last 6 sts, sl1 pw, p5.
Row 7: Using yarn B, knit.
Row 8: Using yarn B, purl.
Row 9: Using yarn A, knit.
Row 10: Using yarn A, purl.
Row 11: Using yarn B, as row 3.
Row 12: Using yarn B, as row 4.
Row 13: Using yarn A, as row 5.
Row 14: Using A, as row 6.
Row 15: Using yarn A, knit

Row 16: Using yarn A, purl.
These 16 rows form the pattern, and are repeated throughout. Continue in pattern for a further 16 rows, ending on a WS row.

Shape armhole
Keeping pattern correct, dec 1 st at armhole edge on next 4 rows (20 sts).
Work 4 rows straight in pattern.

Shape front edge
Dec 1 st at end (front edge) on next and every following 4th row until 14 sts remain. Continue straight until front matches back to shoulder. Bind off.

RIGHT FRONT
Work to match left front reversing shapings for armhole and front edge.

SLEEVES
Make two alike.
Using size US 3 (UK 10/3¼ mm) needles and yarn A cast on 34 sts.
Work in k2, p2 rib for 12 rows increasing 5 sts evenly across last row (39 sts).
Change to US 5 (UK 9/3¾ mm) needles, join in yarn B and work pattern as follows.
Row 1 (RS): Using yarn B, knit.
Row 2: Using yarn B, purl.
Row 3: Using yarn A, k3, *sl1 pw, k3*, rep from * to * to end.
Row 4: Using yarn A, k3, *yf, sl1 pw, yb, K3*, rep from * to * to end.
Row 5: Using yarn B, inc in first st, *sl1 pw, K3*, rep from * to * to last 2 sts, sl1 pw, inc in last st (41 sts).
Row 6: Using yarn B, p2, *sl1 pw, p3*, rep from * to * to last 3 sts, sl1 pw, p2.
Row 7: Using yarn B, knit.

Row 8: Using yarn B, purl.
Row 9: Using yarn A, inc in first st, knit to last st, inc in last st (43 sts).
Row 10: Using yarn A, purl.
Row 11: Using yarn B, k1, *sl1 pw, k3*, rep from * to * to last 2 sts, sl1 pw, k1.
Row 12: Using yarn B, k1, *yf, sl1 pw, yb, k3*, rep from * to * to last 2 sts, yf, sl1 pw, yb, k1.
Row 13: Using yarn A, inc in first st, k2, sl1, *k3, sl1* rep, to last 3 sts. K2, inc in last st.
Row 14: Using yarn A, p4, *sl1 pw, p3*, rep from * to * to last 5 sts, sl1 pw, p4.
Row 15: Using yarn A, knit.
Row 16: Using yarn A, purl.
These 16 rows set the pattern. Taking extra sts into pattern continue to inc 1 st at each end of next and every following 4th row until there are 53 sts on the needle. Continue straight until work measures 7 in (17.5 cm), ending on a WS row.

Shape sleeve top
Keeping pattern correct, dec 1 st at each end of next 4 rows (45 sts). Bind off.

FRONT BAND AND COLLAR

Join shoulder seams.
With RS facing, using US 3 (UK 10/3¼ mm) needles and yarn A, join yarn at base of right front, pick up and knit 81 sts from right front edge, 21 sts from back neck and 80 sts from left front edge (182 sts).
Proceed to shape collar as follows:
Row 1 (WS): (P2, k2) 26 times, turn.
Row 2: P2, (k2, p2) 6 times, turn.
Row 3: K2, (p2, k2) 8 times, turn.
Row 4: P2, (k2, p2) 10 times, turn.
Row 5: K2, (p2, k2) 13 times, turn.
Row 6: P2, (k2, p2) 16 times, turn.

Row 7: K2, p2, *k2, p2*, rep from * to * to end.
Row 8: K2, *p2, k2*, rep from * to * to end.
Work 2 more rows in k2, p2 rib.
Buttonhole row: Rib 4, yrn, work 2tog, *rib 14, yrn, work 2 tog*, rep from * to * once more, rib to end.
Work 7 more rows in rib, then work buttonhole row once more.
Work 3 more rows in rib.
Bind off fairly loosely in rib.

TO FINISH

Work in all ends on pieces. Fold sleeves in half lengthwise, mark center of top, place this marker to correspond with shoulder seam. Stitch sleeves in place. Join side and sleeve seams matching stripes. Sew on buttons firmly to correspond with buttonholes. Fold back collar.

strawberry shoes

Using the softest baby yarn and bright colors, create these super cute shoes for your baby. Worked mainly in stockinette stitch with the addition of a few rows of Fairisle dots to depict strawberry seeds, these can be made by even a novice knitter.

♥♥ Intermediate

● ●

MEASUREMENTS
To fit 3–4 month old baby
Length of foot about $3\frac{1}{2}$ in (9 cm)

MATERIALS
- Patons Fairytale Dreamtime 4 ply, 100% wool (50 g balls; 185 yd/170 m): 1 x 50 g ball shade 0091 Red (R); 1 x 50 g ball shade 2931 Yellow (Y); Oddment of shade 2936 Green
- Oddment of white cotton yarn
- Knitting needles size US 3 (UK 10/$3\frac{1}{4}$ mm)
- US D3 (UK 10/$3\frac{1}{4}$ mm) crochet hook
- 2 x tiny buttons

GAUGE
28 sts x 36 rows measures 4 in (10 cm) square over st st

SPECIAL ABBREVIATIONS
M1 = make a stitch by picking up the strand of yarn between the stitches and knitting into the back of it.

Note: Strand the color not in use across the back of the work, making sure that you don't pull the yarn tight or this will result in puckered work.

● ●

RIGHT SHOE
Using US 3 (UK 10/$3\frac{1}{4}$ mm) needles and yarn R, cast on 48 sts.
Row 1: Knit.
Row 2: (K2, M1, k1) twice, knit to last 6 sts, (k1, M1, k2) twice.
Row 3: Knit.
Repeat the last 2 rows once more (56 sts).
Knit 2 rows.
Next row: K25, (k1, M1) 6 times, knit 25 (62 sts).
Next row: Purl. Joining in and breaking yarn Y as required, work pattern as follows:
Row 1 (RS): K2 R, k1 Y. *k3 R, k1 Y*, rep from * to * to last 3 sts, k3 R.
Using yarn R, work 3 rows in st st.
Row 5: K4 R, k1 Y, *k3 R, k1 Y*, rep from * to * to last 5 sts, k5 R.
Using yarn R, work 3 rows in st st.
Row 9: As row 1.
Using yarn R, work 2 rows in st st. Break R, join in green yarn and purl 1 row.
Next row: K19, (k2tog) 12 times, knit 19 (50 sts).
Next row: P33, turn.
Next row: (K2tog) 8 times, k1, turn.
Next row: P10, turn.
Next row: (K2tog) 5 times, k3, turn.
Next row: Bind off 11 sts, knit to end. ***

Buttonhole band

Next row: K13.

Next row: Cast on 20 sts, knit to end (33 sts).

Buttonhole row: Knit to last 4 sts, yf, k2tog, k2.

Knit 2 rows. Bind off.

Button band

With RS facing, rejoin yarn to remaining 13 sts and work 5 rows in garter stitch. Bind off.

LEFT SHOE

Work as Right Shoe to ***.

Button band

Work 5 rows in garter stitch on these 13 sts. Bind off.

Buttonhole band

With RS facing, rejoin yarn to remaining 13 sts, cast on 20 sts, knit to end (33 sts).

Next row: Knit.

Buttonhole row: K2, k2tog, yf, knit to end.

Knit 2 rows. Bind off.

Flowers

Make two alike.

Using US D3 (UK 10/3¼ mm) crochet hook and yarn Y, make 3 ch, join into a circle with a sl st. Break yarn Y and join in white yarn.

Next round: *5ch, sl st into circle, rep from * 5 times more, join with a sl st. Fasten off.

TO FINISH

Work in all ends neatly. Using a flat seam, join underfoot, heel and back seams. Sew on buttons firmly. Sew flowers on to fronts of shoes using the photograph as a guide. (Make sure they are very securely on in order to eliminate any danger of baby pulling them off.)

teddy hoodie

Knitted in contrasting yarns, this jacket is fairly easy to make, but will take extra concentration when using different yarns for the hood edging. Remember to twist yarns together when changing shades to prevent getting holes in your work.

♥♥♥ Experienced

MEASUREMENTS
To fit 6–12 month old baby
Chest 22 in (56 cm); length from back of neck 12 in (31 cm); sleeve length 6½ in (16 cm)

MATERIALS.
- Sirdar Snuggly DK, 55% nylon/45% acrylic blend (50 g balls; 180 yd/165 m): 2 x 50 g balls shade 344 Oatmeal (A)
- Sirdar Snuggly Tiny Tots DK, 90% acrylic/10% polyester blend (50 g balls; 150 yd/137 m): 3 x 50 g balls shade 957 Stone (B)
- Oddments of brown and black DK for animal appliqué
- Knitting needles size US 5 (UK 9/3¾ mm)
- Knitting needles size US 6 (UK 8/4 mm)
- 5 x animal buttons.

GAUGE
24 st x 28 rows measures 4 in (10 cm) square

ABBREVIATIONS
SS = seed stitch (moss stitch UK) see page 27.

Note: Strand yarns not in use loosely up the side of the work when working st st stripes.

BACK

Using US 5 (UK 9/3¾ mm) needles and yarn A, cast on 67 sts. Work in seed stitch as follows:
Row 1 (RS): K1, *p1, k1*, rep from * to * to end.
Row 2: K1, *p1, k1*, rep from * to * to end.
These 2 rows form seed stitch.
Continue in seed st for a further 10 rows, ending on a WS row.
Change to US 6 (UK 8/4 mm) needles, st st and work in st st stripes as follows: 6 rows in yarn B, 6 rows in yarn A.
Continue in st st stripes for a further 24 rows, ending on last row of 6th stripe. Work will measure approx. 6 in (15 cm) in length.
Adjust length here if needed. But make sure that you end each piece of the jacket on the same row to facilitate continuity of the pattern when sewing up.
Shape raglans
Keeping stripes correct bind off 1 st at beg of next 2 rows (65 sts)
Next row: K2, sl1, k1, psso, knit to last 4 sts, k2tog, k2.
Next row: Purl.
Repeat the last 2 rows until 23 sts remain. Bind off.

LEFT FRONT

Using US 5 (UK 9/3¾ mm) needles and yarn A, cast on 39 sts.

Work in seed stitch as for back for 11 rows.

Row 12: Seed stitch across first 8 sts, slip these stitches onto a safety pin for front band. Seed stitch to end (31 sts).

Change to US 6 (UK 8/4 mm) needles, and work in st st stripes as for back until work measures the same as back to raglan shaping, ending on a WS row.

Shape raglans

Keeping stripes correct, bind off 1 st at beg of next row (30 sts).

Purl 1 row.

Next row: K2, sl1, k1, psso, knit to end.

Next row: Purl.

Repeat the last 2 rows until 13 sts remain, ending on a RS row.

Shape neck

Row 1 (WS): Bind off 2 sts, purl to end.

Row 2: K2, sl1, k1, psso, knit to last 2 st, k2tog.

Row 3: P2tog, purl to end.

Repeat rows 2 and 3 once more (5 sts).

Next row: Purl.

Next row: K1, sl1, psso (2 sts).

Next row: Purl.

Next row: Sl1, k1, psso and fasten off

RIGHT FRONT

Using US 5 (UK 9/3¾ mm) needles and yarn A cast on 39 sts.

Work in seed stitch as for back for 6 rows.

Next row: (Make buttonhole), seed stitch 3 sts, bind off 2 sts, seed stitch to end.

Next row: Seed stitch to end but cast on 2 sts above the bind off sts of previous row.

Work in seed stitch for 2 more rows.

Row 11: Seed stitch 8 sts, slip onto a safety pin for front border, seed stitch to end (31 sts).

Row 12: Seed stitch to end.

Change to US 6 (UK 8/4 mm) needles and work to match left front reversing shapings, working 1 row more before start of raglan shaping and working k2tog instead of sl1, k1, psso at raglan shaping until 14 sts remain, ending on a WS row.

Shape neck

Row 1 (RS): Bind off 2 sts, knit to last 4 st, k2tog, k2.

Row 2: Purl.

Row 3: K2tog, knit to last 4 sts, k2tog, k2.

Row 4: Purl.

Repeat rows 3 and 4 once more (5 sts).

Next row: K3tog, k2 (3 sts).

Next row: Purl.

Next row: K2tog, k1 (2 sts).

Next row: Purl.

Next row: K2tog and fasten off.

SLEEVES

Make two alike.

Using US 5 (UK 9/3¾ mm) needles and yarn A, cast on 33 sts.

Work seed stitch as for back for 18 rows.

Change to US 6 (UK 8/4 mm) needles, and work in st st stripes as before, increasing 1 st at each end of the needle on the 5th row and then every following 6th row, until there are 43 sts.

Continue Straight for 7 rows, ending on last row of 6th stripe. Work will measure approx. 6½ in (16 cm). Adjust length here to match back if required.

Shape raglans

Keeping stripes correct, bind off 1 stitch at beg of next 2 rows (31 sts).

Row 3: K2, sl1, k1, psso, to last 4 sts, k2tog, k2.
Row 4: Purl.
Row 5: Knit.
Row 6: Purl.
Repeat the last 4 rows 4 times more, then rep rows 3 and 4 only until 9 sts remain. Bind off.

HOOD

Using US 6 (UK 8/4 mm) needles and yarn B cast on 42 sts, join in A and cast on 13 sts (55 sts).
Work in st st stripes as before, but keeping 13 sts at end of row in seed stitch as follows:
Note: Twist yarns together when changing to stop holes and use a separate ball of yarn A when needed.
Row 1 (RS): Using yarn B, k42 sts, using yarn A seed stitch 13 sts.
Row 2: Using yarn A, seed stitch 13, using yarn B, p42.
Continue, working stripes of yarn A and B as before, keeping the 13 sts seed stitch border correct.
When you have completed 15 stripes in all bind off.

Button and buttonhole bands

Using US 5 (UK 9/3¾ mm) needles and yarn A return to stitches on stitch holder of left front. Continue in seed stitch until band, when slightly stretched fits up side of left front to neck shaping. Bind off in pattern. Using US 5 (UK 9/3¾ mm) needles, return to stitches on holder of right front. Continue in seed stitch, working buttonholes approximately 20 rows between until 5 button holes in all have been worked. Work 4 more rows. Bind off.

TEDDY MOTIF
Face
Worked in garter stitch.

Using US 5 (UK 9/3¾ mm) needles and brown yarn, cast on 8 sts. Knit 2 rows.
Inc 1 st at each end of next and every following alt row until there are 16 sts.
Knit 10 rows.
Dec 1 st at each end of next and every following alt row until there are 10 sts remaining.
Knit 2 rows and bind off.

Mask

Using US 5 (UK 9/3¾ mm) needles and yarn A, cast on 2 sts.
Next row: Purl.
Continue in st st and inc 1 st at each end of next and every following alt row until there are 12 sts.
Work 5 rows in st st, ending on a purl row.
Next row: K2tog, k2, k2tog, turn.
Next row: P4.
Next row: (K2tog) twice, pass first st over second st and fasten off.
With RS facing, rejoin yarn to remaining 6 sts, and complete to match first side.

Muzzle

Using US 5 (UK 9/3¾ mm) needles and yarn A, cast on 3 sts.
Next row: Purl.
Continue in st st and inc 1 st at each end of next and every following alt row until you have 11 sts, ending on a purl row.
Dec 1 st at each end of next and every following alt row until 3 sts remain. Bind off.

Ears

Make two alike.
Using US 5 (UK 9/3¾ mm) needles and brown yarn, cast on 3 sts. Knit 1 row.
Inc 1 st at each end of next row (5 sts).
Knit 4 rows.
Dec 1 st at each end of next row (3 sts).
Knit 1 row. Bind off.

TO FINISH

Work all ends in neatly. Join sleeves to back and fronts matching stripes as you sew. Join side and sleeve seams, again matching stripes. Fold front edge of hood in half on to right side, catch down at each side. Stitch front bands in place stretching slightly to give a neat finish. Sew on buttons to correspond with button holes.

Join back seam of hood. Pin hood around neck edge, beginning and ending 4 stitches in from each front edge of jacket. Sew in place.

Take head section of motif and lay flat. Sew mask onto head, easing slightly to get a nice shape. Sew muzzle sideways onto base of mask, add a tiny bit of yarn as stuffing to pad out. Sew ears to either side of head, pleating at the base to give shape. Embroider eyes, nose and mouth with black yarn using the photograph as a guide. Sew the motif very firmly to jacket front.

nursery laundry bag

A soft cotton-rich yarn is used to make this delightful laundry bag for the nursery.
An easy textured stitch is used for the main body of the bag and an intarsia design
square is worked separately and stitched onto the front.

♥♥ Intermediate

MEASUREMENTS
$18\frac{1}{2}$ x $19\frac{1}{2}$ in (49 x 50 cm)

MATERIALS
- Rico Baby Soft Cotton DK, 50% cotton/50% acrylic
  (50 g balls; 136 yd/125 m): 7 x 50 g balls shade 016
  Arctic Blue (A); 2 x 50 g balls shade 007 Blue (B);
  2 x 50 g balls shade 012 Berry (C)
- Knitting needles size US 6 (UK 8/4 mm)

GAUGE
20 sts x 28 rows measures 4 in (10 cm) square over st st

BACK AND FRONT
Make two alike.
Using US 6 (UK 8/4 mm) needles and yarn A, cast on
95 sts.
Next row: Purl.
Now work pattern as follows:
Row 1 (RS): K1,*bring yarn to front, sl1, take yarn to
back, k1*, rep from * to * to end.
Row 2: Purl.
Row 3: K2, *bring yarn to front, sl1, take yarn to back,
k1*, rep from * to * to last st, k1.
Row 4: Purl.
These 4 rows form the pattern and are repeated
throughout.
Continue in pattern as set until work measures
$19\frac{1}{2}$ in (50 cm) ending on a purl row. Break yarn A.
Change to yarn B and work in st st for 6 rows. Break
yarn B and join in yarn C and work a further 6 rows.
Break yarn C and join in yarn B, and work a further 6
rows. Bind off.

Motif square
Using US 6 (UK 8/4 mm) needles and yarn A, cast on
39 sts.
Knit 3 rows in garter stitch.
Next row (RS): Knit.
Next row: K4, p31, k4.

Repeat the last 2 rows 4 times more.
Note: When working boat motif from chart, use separate balls of yarn for each color and do not strand yarn across back of work. Odd rows knit from right to left and even rows purl from left to right.
Work boat motif from chart as follows:
Row 1 (RS): K7, work 25 sts as row 1 of chart, k7.
Row 2: K4, p3, work 25 sts as row 2 of chart, p3, k4.
These two rows set position of chart. Continue as set until 29 rows of chart have been worked. Break off yarns B and C and continue in yarn A only.
Work 11 rows in yarn A as st st, then work 3 rows in garter stitch, ending on a WS row. Bind off.

Flags

Work in garter stitch and make 5 (1 in yarn A, 2 in yarn B and 2 in yarn C). Using appropriate shade and US 6 (UK 8/4 mm) needles, cast on 21 sts.
Knit 4 rows.
Dec 1 st at beg of every row until 3 sts remain.
Next row: Sl1, k1, psso and fasten off.

Rope tie

Make a long twisted cord, about 59 in (150 cm) long (see page 20). Secure both ends. Thread through top of bag, stitch the ends together and fray into a tassle.

TO FINISH

Work in all ends. Place the square in the center of front piece, and sew neatly in place. With right sides facing inside, join back and front together along three sides, leaving top section open. Fold back striped edging in half, catch down all around, leaving an opening to thread in cord. Sew the flags in place along the bottom edge of bag, using the photograph as a guide.

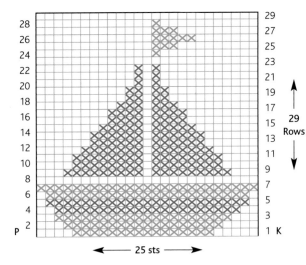

29 Rows

teddy bear hat

Who can resist this cute little teddy bear hat! The basic hat is knitted in the softest baby yarn then the facial features are knitted separately and sewn on afterwards. A twisted cord, sewn firmly onto each ear flap will hold the hat in place.

♥♥ Intermediate

MEASUREMENTS
To fit 3–6 month old baby

MATERIALS
- Sirdar Snuggly DK, 55% nylon/45% acrylic (50 g balls; 191 yd/175 m): 1 x 50 g ball shade 321 Pastel Blue 321; 1 x 50 g ball shade 251 White; Oddment of shade 312 Black for eyes
- Knitting needles size US 5 (UK 9/3¾ mm)

GAUGE
20 sts x 28 rows measures 4 in (10 cm) square over st st

EAR FLAPS
Make two alike.
Using US 5 (UK 9/3¾ mm) needles and blue yarn, cast on 6 sts.
Row 1: Knit.
Row 2: Inc in first st, knit to last 2 sts, inc in next st, k1.
Repeat last row until there are 22 st on the needle, do not bind off, slip sts onto a holder.

HAT
Using US 5 (UK 9/3¾ mm) needles and blue yarn, cast on 9 sts, knit across sts of one earflap, turn and cast on 22 sts, knit across sts from second earflap, turn and cast on 9 sts (84 sts).
Work in garter stitch across all stitches for 6 rows. Change to st st and work 26 rows ending on a purl row.
Shape top
Row 1: K3, (k2tog, k4) 13 times, k2tog, k1 (70 sts).
Row 2: Purl.
Row 3: K2, (k2tog, k3) 13 times, k2tog, k1 (56 sts).
Row 4: Purl.
Row 5: K1, (k2tog, k2) 13 times, k2tog, k1 (42 sts).
Row 6: Purl.
Row 7: (K2tog, k1) 14 times (28 sts).
Row 8: Purl.
Row 9: (K2tog) 14 times (14 sts).
Break yarn and run through remaining sts, draw up tight and secure.

MUZZLE
Using US 5 (UK 9/3¾ mm) needles and white yarn, cast on 5 sts.
Knit 2 rows.
Inc 1 st each end of next and every following alt row until there are 11 sts.

Knit 6 rows.
Dec 1 st each end of next and every following alt row until 5 sts remain.
Knit 2 rows. Bind off.

EARS
Outer ears
Make two alike.
Using US 5 (UK 9/3¾ mm) needles and white yarn cast on 10 sts. Knit 2 rows.
Next row: Inc in each of next 3 sts, k4, inc in each of last 3 sts (16 sts).
Knit 6 rows.
Dec 1 st each end of next and every following alt row until 10 sts remain.
Next row: (K2tog) 5 times (5 sts). Bind off.

Inner ears
Make two alike.
Using US 5 (UK 9/3¾ mm) needles and blue yarn, cast on 10 sts. Knit 2 rows.
Next row: Inc in each of next 2 sts, k6, inc in each of last 2 sts (14 sts).
Knit 4 rows.
Dec 1 st each end of next and every following alt row until 8 sts remain.
Next row: (K2tog) 4 times (4 sts). Bind off.

EYES
Outer eyes
Make two alike.
Using US 5 (UK 9/3¾ mm) needles and and black yarn, cast on 3 sts.
Row 1: Knit.
Row 2: Inc in first st, k1, inc in last st (5 sts).
Knit 3 rows.

Dec 1 st each end of next row.
Knit 1 row.
Next row: Sl1, k2tog, psso and fasten off.

Inner eyes
Make two.
Using US 5 (UK 9/3¾ mm) needles and and black yarn, cast on 3 sts.
Row 1: Knit.
Row 2: Inc in first st, k1, inc in last st (5 sts)
Row 3: Knit.
Row 4: K2tog, k1, k2tog (3 sts).
Row 5: Knit.
Row 6: Sl1, k2tog, psso and fasten off.

TO FINISH
Work in all ends and sew seam of hat. Fold hat with seam at the center back. Sew ears together in pairs of one outer and one inner, pleat at the base to give shape, sew onto either side of crown. Take muzzle and place on center front of hat a little above garter stitch. Pad lightly to give the bear a snout, sew in place. Using blue yarn, stitch nose and mouth into muzzle, using the photograph as a guide. Sew eyes together, placing the inner eye on top of the outer eye, and catch in place just above the muzzle. Using white yarn, stitch highlight onto eyes, using the photograph as guide. Make two twisted cords (see page 20 for instructions), using blue yarn and stitch securely to each flap.

just rosy

A delicate lacy pattern and soft yarn are used to make a special set for a tiny baby. Although the pattern looks complicated, it is an 8-row repeat so will not be too difficult to follow. Knitted roses and leaves add a sweet finishing touch.

♥♥♥ Experienced

MEASUREMENTS
To fit newborn–3 month old baby

MATERIALS
- Patons Fairytale 4ply baby yarn, 40% nylon/60% acrylic (50 g balls; 161 yd/147m): 1 x 50 g ball shade 4371 Pink (B); 2 x 50 g balls shade 4300 White (A); Oddments of shade 4374 Green
- Knitting needles size US 3 (UK 10/3¼ mm)
- Knitting needles size US 5 (UK 9/3¾ mm)
- 2 yd (2 m) narrow white satin ribbon
- Small white button

GAUGE
20 sts x 28 rows measures 4 in (10 cm) square over st st

BONNET
Using US 3 (UK 10/3¼ mm) needles and pink yarn, cast on 85 st.
Work 6 rows in garter stitch.
Change to US 5 (UK 9/3¾ mm) needles and white yarn and work pattern as follows:

Row 1: (RS) K1, *yf, sl1, k2tog, psso, k5*, repeat from * to * to last 4 sts, yf, sl1, k2tog, psso, yf, k1.
Row 2 and every following alternate row: Purl.
Row 3: As row 1.
Row 5: K4, *yf, sl1, k1, psso, k1, k2tog, yf, k3*, rep from * to * to last st, k1.
Row 7: K1, *yf, sl1, k2tog, psso, yf, k1*, rep from * to * to end.
Row 8: Purl.
These 8 rows form the pattern and are repeated throughout.
Repeat these 8 rows 3 times more, decreasing 1 st in the center of the last row (84 sts).
Now continue in st st until work measures 4½ in (11.5 cm), ending on a purl row.
Shape crown
Row 1: (K10, k2tog) 7 times.
Row 2 and every following alternate row: Purl.
Row 3: (K9, k2tog) 7 times.
Row 5: (K8, k2tog) 7 times.
Continue to decrease in this way working 1 less st before k2tog until 14 sts remain.
Break yarn and run through remaining stitches, draw up tight and secure.
Button strap
Using US 3 (UK 10/3¼ mm) needles and white yarn cast on 5 sts.
Work 2 rows in garter stitch.

Work in pattern as follows:

Row 1: K2, yf, k2tog, k1.

Rows 2–4: Knit.

Rep these 4 rows 13 times more, then rows 1 and 2 once more.

Next row: K2tog, k1, k2tog (3 sts).

Next row: Knit.

Next row: K3tog and fasten off.

MITTENS

Make two alike. Using US 3 (UK 10/3¼ mm) needles and pink yarn cast on 37 st.

Work 3 rows in garter stitch.

Break pink yarn and join in white yarn; work pattern as follows:

Row 1 (RS): K1, *yf, sl1, k2tog, psso, k5*, rep from * to * to last 4 sts, yf, sl1, k2tog, psso, yf, k1.

Row 2 and every following alternate row: Purl.

Row 3: As row 1.

Row 5: K4, *yf, sl1, k1, psso, k1, k2tog, yf, k3*, repeat from * to * to last st, k1.

Row 7: K1, *yf, sl1, k2tog, psso, yf, k1*, repeat from * to * to end.

Row 8: Purl.

These 8 rows form the pattern and are repeated throughout.

Repeat these 8 rows once more.

Work 4 rows in st st, ending on a purl row.

Next row: (Make eyelets) K1, *yf, k2tog*, rep from * to * to end.

Next row: Purl decreasing 3 sts evenly across row (34 sts).

Continue in st st until work measures 2½ in (6 cm), ending on a purl row.

Shape top

Row 1: K1, (k2tog tbl, k12, k2tog) twice, k1 (30 sts).

Row 2 and every following alternate row: Purl.

Row 3: K1, (k2tog tbl, k10, k2tog) twice, k1 (26 sts).

Row 5: K1, (k2tog tbl, k8, k2tog) twice, k1 (22 sts).

Row 7: K1, (k2tog,tbl, k6, k2tog) twice, k1 (18 sts).

Row 8: Purl. Bind off.

BOOTIES

Make two alike.

Using US 3 (UK 10/3¼ mm) needles and pink yarn, cast on 37 sts.

Work 3 rows in garter stitch.

Break pink and join in white yarn. Work pattern as follows:

Row 1 (RS): K1, *yf, sl1, k2tog, psso, k5*, rep from * to * to last 4 sts, yf, sl1, k2tog, psso, yf, k1.

Row 2 and every following alternate row: Purl.

Row 3: As row 1.

Row 5: K4, *yf, sl1, k1, psso, k1, k2tog, yf, k3*, rep from * to * to last st, k1.

Row 7: K1, *yf, sl1, k2tog, psso, yf, k1*, rep from * to * to end.

Row 8: Purl.

These 8 rows form the pattern and are repeated throughout. Repeat these 8 rows twice more.

Shape instep
Next row: K24, turn.
Next row: P11, turn.
Continue on these 11 sts and work 18 rows in st st, ending on a purl row. Break yarn.

Work foot
With right side facing pick up and knit 10 sts along side of instep, knit 11 sts from instep, pick up and knit 10 sts along other side of instep, knit across remaining 13 sts (57 sts).
Work 15 rows in garter stitch, ending on a WS row.

Shape foot
Row 1: K1, *K2tog tbl, k23, K2tog, k1*, rep from * to * to end (53 sts).
Row 2: Knit.
Row 3: K1, *K2tog tbl, k21, K2tog, k1*, rep from * to * to end (49 sts).
Row 4: Knit.
Row 5: K1, *K2tog tbl, k19, K2tog, k1*, rep from * to * to end (45 sts).
Row 6: Knit. Bind off.

ROSES AND LEAVES
Large rose
Make two alike.
Using US 3 (UK 10/3¼ mm) needles and pink yarn, cast on 25 sts.
Row 1: Knit.
Row 2: Knit twice into each st across row (50 sts). Bind off. Coil work tightly into a rose shape and secure with a few stitches.

Large leaf
Make two alike. Using US 3 (UK 10/3¼ mm) needles and green yarn cast on 3 sts.
Row 1: Purl.
Row 2: K1, inc in next st, k1 (4 sts).
Row 3: Knit.
Row 4: inc in first st, k2, inc in last st.
Work 4 rows garter stitch.
Dec 1 st at each end of next 2 rows (2 sts).
Next row: K2tog and fasten off.

Small rose
Make four alike. Using US 3 (UK 10/3¼ mm) needles and pink yarn cast on 18 sts.
Row 1: Knit.
Row 2: Knit twice into each st across row (36 sts). Cast off. Coil work tightly into a rose shape and secure with a few stitches.

Small leaf
Make four alike. Using US 3 (UK 10/3¼ mm) needles and green yarn, cast on 3 sts.
Row 1: Purl.
Row 2: K1, inc in next st, k1 (4 sts).
Work 4 rows in garter stitch.
Dec 1 st at each end of next row.
Next row: K2tog and fasten off.

TO FINISH
Sew in all ends neatly. Join back seam of bonnet. Attach a rose and leaf on either side of bonnet. Sew strap in place catching one side to the bonnet firmly, sew button to other side. Use button on strap to adjust to fit. Sew side seams of mittens. Thread ribbon through holes at wrist and tie in bows. Attach a rose and leaf to the back of mitten. Sew back and sole seam of booties. Thread ribbon through last hole row of lacy pattern at ankle, tie in a neat bow. Attach rose and leaf on each bootie as in photograph.

Suppliers

Knitting Fever Inc.
315 Bayview Ave.
Amityville, NY 11701
516-546-3600
www.knittingfever.com

Westminster Fibers
165 Ledge Street
Nashua, NH 03063
www.westminsterfibers.com

Yarn Market
888-996-9276
www.yarnmarket.com

WEBS – America's Yarn Store
800-367-9327
customerservice@yarn.com
www.yarn.com

Many other yarn suppliers and useful
information can be found on the
internet or try your local yarn shop
or a craft store near you.